Nuzi, Women's Rights and Hurrian Ethnicity And Other Academic Essays

**Hermit Kingdom Studies
in Identity and Society 1**

Nuzi, Women's Rights and Hurrian Ethnicity And Other Academic Essays

Heerak Christian Kim

The Hermit Kingdom Press
Cheltenham ♦ Seoul ♦ Bangalore ♦ Cebu

Nuzi, Women's Rights and Hurrian Ethnicity
And Other Academic Essays

Copyright © 2006 by Heerak Christian Kim

All rights reserved. No part of this book may be reproduced in any form or by any means, electronic or mechanical, including photocopying, recording, or by any information storage and retrieval system (including computer files in any form), without permission in writing from the publisher.

Hardcover: ISBN 1-59689-049-5
Paperback: ISBN 1-59689-050-9
E-Book: ISBN 1-59689-051-7

Write-To Address:

| The Hermit Kingdom Press
3741 Walnut Street, Suite 407
Philadelphia, PA 19104
United States of America
info@TheHermitKingdomPress.com |
|---|

Library of Congress Cataloging-in-Publication Data

Kim, H. C. (Heerak Christian)
  Nuzi, women's rights, and Hurrian ethnicity, and other academic essays / Heerak Christian Kim.
      p. cm. -- (Hermit Kingdom studies in identity and society ; 1)
  ISBN 1-59689-049-5 (hardcover : alk. paper) -- ISBN 1-59689-050-9 (pbk. : alk. paper)
  1. Theology. 2. Church history. I. Title. II. Series.
  BT21.3.K56 2006
  200.9--dc22
                                        2005036325

In Memory of

Rosa Parks (1913-2005)

Whose Courage

Changed the World for Better

"Whatever my individual desires were to be free, I was not alone. There were many others who felt the same way."

Rosa Parks

Contents

Genesis 17, P, and the Lasting Impact of the Covenantal Seal of Olam
෴ 1 ෴

Nuzi, Women's Rights, and Hurrian Ethnicity: Land Ownership and Adoption of Women as a Key to Unlocking the Past
෴ 21 ෴

Augustus' Manipulation of Traditional Roman Religion
෴ 44 ෴

A Review of Caroline Walker Bynum's *Holy Feast and Holy Fast: The Religious Significance of Food to Medieval Women*
෴ 65 ෴

Syriac Spirituality: Clothing and Nakedness as Symbolic Reality
෴ 75 ෴

Marriage in the Qumran Community
෴ 109 ෴

Contents

Philo of Alexandria's Portrait of Moses
ം 124 ഉം

A Paradigmatic Shift in the Redemptive
Medium of the Law:
Paul's Thoughts as a Bridge
ം 144 ഉം

Investiture Contest as a Struggle
for Right Order in the World:
A Precis of Gerd Tellenbach's
*Church, State and Christian Society at the Time of the
Investiture Controversy*
ം 178 ഉം

Preface

This book represents research conducted on a professional academic level for fifteen years. During that period, I have had the pleasure of working with some of the leading academics in the world in the fields of Ancient Near Eastern Studies, History of Christianity, New Testament Studies, Jewish Studies, Qumran Studies, and Medieval Studies. All the articles in this volume represent original research on my part, and I hope that they will be helpful in advancing knowledge and thinking about history, religion, and identity.

I have been blessed with various opportunities that enhanced my development as a scholar and I would like to mention them here. I would like to thank The Lady Davis Foundation for awarding me the Lady Davis Fellowship for the 1996-97 academic year. It is a great honor to be a Lady Davis Fellow and to belong to a group of elite scholars around the world who have held the same honor.

Preface

I would also like to thank my students at Asia Evangelical College and Seminary in Bangalore, India, who have helped me think through some research issues in a more practical ways. Majority my students are masters level students, pursuing the M.Div. or M.A.R. degree. I hope that I have encouraged them and that they will become important theology scholars and knowledgeable ministers in Christian churches in India and all over the world.

I would also like to thank American undergraduate students I had the pleasure of teaching at the University of California, Los Angeles in history courses on religion and western civilization. Thanks also are in order for the undergraduate students I had the pleasure of teaching in Judaic Studies courses at Brown University. My three hours per week office hours were always packed with inquisitive undergraduate students who wanted to understand history and the past, and I had to add few more hours every week to accommodate the interested undergraduate students seeking knowledge and advice. Their great interest in the materials being taught encouraged me to develop further as a scholar who wants to contribute to advancement of knowledge.

It's wonderful to see that one of my students at UCLA, Tim Kao, is currently pursuing a Ph.D. in Old Testament studies at Oxford University's Theology department. I hope that he will become a very important scholar in the field of biblical studies. He is the only one who earned the grade of "A+" that year, so I am sure that he will distinguish himself.

NUZI, WOMEN'S RIGHTS AND
HURRIAN ETHNICITY AND OTHER
ACADEMIC ESSAYS

"Genesis 17, P, and the Lasting Impact of the Covenantal Seal of *Olam*"[1]

Genesis 17 is a very important document for understanding the Abrahamic covenant in the Old Testament and its import for Israelite history. With a distinctive stamp of the priestly writer (P), Genesis 17 represents a developed stage in the Israelite understanding of the covenant between God and Abraham, and by extension between God and Israelites. In fact, the Abrahamic covenant as preserved in Genesis 17 portrays the hopes and fears of the exilic period. Particularly, the concern of P to declare God as righteous and Israelites as responsible to the covenant is patently visible. This is evident in the covenant seal of עולם. עולם is found in four places in Genesis 17 – in verses 7, 8, 13, and 19 – and it represents a crystallized legal seal that functions as signing the covenant and binding the parties in the covenant to legal obligation. The distinctive stamp of P is evident in Genesis 17, particularly seen in comparison to Genesis 15, another document containing the portrayal of the Abrahamic covenant. Post-exilic writings indicate the lasting impact of עולם

---

[1] This academic paper was delivered on Monday, June 27, 2005, at the Pentateuch Section of the International Society of Biblical Literature academic conference held in Singapore. The SBL conference was historic in that it was the first time in the academic society's history to hold the global academic conference in Asia. I would like to thank Professor Alan Hauser, who presided the section, for his helpful comments and kind words of praise.

as a covenantal seal and a symbol of the Abrahamic covenant.

It is not difficult to see that the concept of forever is prominently attached to the covenant. In the Biblical text, the term is frequently used in covenant myth passages. Genesis 17, which is considered to be recounting the story of covenant-making in the earliest stages – that of the time of Abraham, prominently employs the term "forever" in key places. The term is attested in verses 7, 8, 13, and 19.

In Genesis 17:7, God promises to be Abraham's God and the God of Abraham's descendants for generations to come and this is to be an everlasting covenant. The concept of "forever" functions as a seal to the important covenant. God has bound himself to the everlasting covenant forever.

In Genesis 17:8, God promises to give the whole land of Canaan as an everlasting possession for Abraham and his descendants. This promise is understood to be a part of the everlasting covenant. The concept of "forever" functions to endorse the permanency of the covenant. Like Genesis 17:8, the term "forever" therefore comes to be attached to the very identity of the covenant itself. There is a qualifier in Genesis 17:8 that God will be the God of their descendants. In a sense, this is the condition for the responsibility of Abraham's descendants to bind God to fulfil his role in the everlasting covenant. There is an implicit understanding that Israelites must worship Yahweh as their God.

Genesis 17:13 brings out the responsibilities of Abraham's descendants for the satisfaction of the everlasting covenant. Every male of Abraham's descendants and their households had to be circumcised. This obligation for circumcision is a part of the everlasting covenant. The term "forever" again becomes a type of seal to emphasize the gravity of the covenant. The seriousness of the covenant obligation of circumcision is highlighted in Genesis 17:4. The verse commands that any male who is not circumcised must be expelled from the community of Abraham's descendants because he has broken the covenant.

Genesis 17:19 basically reinforces the idea of the everlasting covenant. Repeating some ideas found in Genesis 17:7, God promises to establish an everlasting covenant with Isaac and his descendants. Verse 19, therefore, functions to reaffirm the covenantal promise of Genesis 17:7. The term "forever" is used as a type of seal related to the identity of the serious covenant.

One sees that "forever, everlasting" in all four attestations acts as a crucial element in the emphasis of the clauses of the covenant. It is a part of the everlasting covenant that God will be the God of Israel. It is a part of the everlasting covenant that God will give Israelites their land. It is a part of the everlasting covenant that Israelites must circumcise for their part in the covenantal agreement.[2] The

---

[2] Regarding the covenantal obligation of circumcision on Abraham/Israel's part, Paul R. Williamson writes: "Failure to conform to this ritual requirement was considered a breach of the covenant" (Paul R. Williamson, *Abraham, Israel and the Nations: The Patriarchal Promise and its Covenantal Development in Genesis* <Sheffield: Sheffield Academic Press, 2000>, p. 182). V. P. Hamilton writes also writes: "The designation of

everlasting nature of the covenant is emphasized in reiterating the covenant with Abraham as a covenant also made with Isaac.[3] Thus, in a sense "forever, everlasting" functions as a covenantal seal. Paul R. Williamson points out the significance of עולם in Genesis 17: "It is used of the covenant itself; the covenant, and by implication, the special relationship established by it, is said to be 'everlasting.' Thus it would appear that this is another feature which is expressly applied to the actual covenant between God and Abraham (and not simply to a promissory element of it) for the first time in Genesis 17."[4]

It is not surprising why the concept of "forever" plays such a crucial role in the covenant with Abraham as found in Genesis 17 when one looks at the background of Genesis 17. Most scholars agree that Genesis 17 is a P document from the Exile. Sean E. McEvenue emphatically claims that

---

circumcision itself as a covenant is a synecdoche for covenantal obligation" (V. P. Hamilton, *The Book of Genesis, Chapters 1-17* <Grand Rapids: Eerdmans, 1990>, p. 470).

[3] Thomas L. Thompson notes that the specific mention of establishing God's covenant with Isaac in Genesis 17:19, 21 functions as a narrative transition that harmonizes disparate traditions introduced in Genesis 15-16. It effectively isolates Ishmael from the covenant despite previous blessings and his being circumcised (Thomas L. Thompson, *The Origin Tradition of Ancient Israel: The Literary Formation of Genesis and Exodus 1-23* <Sheffield: Sheffield Academic Press, 1987>, pp. 90-91).

[4] Williamson, *Abraham, Israel and the Nations*, p. 172. See also J. H. Sailhamer, *The Pentateuch as Narrative: A Biblical Theological Commentary* (Grand Rapids: Zondervan, 1992), p. 158.

Genesis 17 is "purely priestly in style."[5] John Van Seters writes: "The group associated with Genesis 17 is generally recognized by all the literary critics as the work of P...."[6] Gerhard Von Rad argues that Genesis 17 is a P document that represents P's holistic understanding of the Abrahamic covenant based on various priestly (P) traditions.[7]

The fact of the P character of Genesis 17 is important for understanding why "forever" functions as a covenantal seal. The Priestly writer, or P, is from the Exile. Thus, P exhibits hopes and fears of the exilic period. The Exile was a traumatic experience for the Israelites. The fact that Israelites were kicked out of the land of Israel, which they perceived as a God-given possession, made many doubt the covenant. Van Seters writes: "The exile was proof that the covenantal relationship was broken, and with it the legitimate claim to the land."[8] Not only that, many Israelites began to doubt that the God of Abraham was still their God the Exile continued for years and years. It was in this period of doubt that P stepped in to reassure Israelites that the God of Abraham was still their God and that the covenant was still in force. McEvenue writes: "The priestly writer, then, must be imagined among the exiles, some of whom are ready to abandon Yahweh, and their heritage, in favour of Babylon's gods, culture,

---

[5] Sean E. McEvenue, *The Narrative Style of the Priestly Writer* (Rome: Biblical Institute Press, 1971), 19.
[6] John Van Seters, *Abraham in History and Tradition* (New Haven: Yale University Press, 1975), 270.
[7] Gerhard Von Rad, *Genesis: A Commentary*, trans. John H. Marks (London: SCM Press Ltd, 1961), 192.
[8] Van Seters, *Abraham in History and Tradition*, 265.

and prosperity.... He sets about to write a theology of hope for the exiles...."[9] Thus, P used the covenantal seal of "forever" to sign, in essence, each clause of the covenant. It was everlasting covenant that the God of Abraham would be the God of Abraham's descendants. It was everlasting covenant that the land of Canaan would belong to them.[10] Thus, despite the fact that they were in Exile, Israelites could look forward to the everlasting covenant and its promises that were still in effect. In a sense, therefore, P emphasized the hope of the covenant. Claus Westermann writes: "Israel is alive because God promised Abraham that he would be his God. The covenant of God with Abraham described by P in Gen. 17 is then an interpretation from the time of the exile, and means in reality the covenant of Yahweh with Israel."[11] Thus, much of the covenant account in Genesis 17 outlines the way P wanted to portray the Abrahamic Covenant to Israelites at the time of the Exile. The obligations of God to Israelites were emphasized to give hope. And the covenantal elements were signed, in effect, with the literary seal of "forever."

The covenantal seal of "forever" signed every clause of the covenant attached to God's obligations to the covenant. But it was not limited to the

---

[9] McEvenue, *The Narrative Style of the Priestly Writer*, 181-182.
[10] McAvenue argues that P indicates that the promise of land was intended for Israelites and not for Abraham (McEvenue, *The Narrative Style of the Priestly Writer*, 166). This is understandable iven the Sitz im Leben of the composition.
[11] Claus Westermann, *Genesis 12-36: A Commentary*, trans. John J. Scullion (Minneapolis: Augsburg Publishing House, 1985), 113.

covenantal clauses regarding God's obligations. In fact, the covenantal seal of "forever" signed the clause outlining the obligations of Israelites to the covenant. It was an everlasting covenant that Israelites circumcise their children.[12] Williamson emphasizes the role of human obligation in the covenant as recorded in Genesis 17: "The central focus in this text is the connection between the covenant promise(s) and the covenant obligations imposed upon Abraham by God, especially the requirement of circumcision."[13] In a sense, therefore, P provided an explanation for why Israelites were in Exile. It was not that the God of Abraham was unfaithful to his covenant obligations. Rather, it was the disregard for their covenantal obligations that Israelites were in Exile.

The reminder of the covenantal obligations of Israelites, therefore, had three functions. First, it reassured the Israelites that the everlasting covenant was valid and still in effect. God would fulfil his part if Israelites fulfilled their part. Second, it worked to encourage the Israelites to proactively observe their obligations in the covenant.[14] They should not give

---

[12] Circumcision as an ethnic identity marker certainly makes sense in the period of the Exile when Israelites were displaced. Van Seters argues that there is a direct link with patriarchal promises. Van Seters writes: "This concern with ethnic descent and racial purity becomes increasingly important in the exile and post-exilic periods because it goes hand-in-hand with the patriarchal promises" (Van Seters, *Abraham in History and Tradition*, 278).
[13] Williamson, *Abraham, Israel and the Nations*, p. 149.
[14] G. J. Wenham writes that the rite of circumcision "is the sign of the covenant, which reminds its possessor of his obligations

up hope and capitulate to the conditions of the Exile. Thirdly, it forced the priestly agenda for cultic observance. P was interested in propping up the Jerusalem Temple cult. There was hope in the Exile that the Jerusalem Temple would be rebuilt, and P worked to focus Israelites' thoughts onto cultic observance. Williamson writes regarding the import of the ritual of circumcision: "This chapter is alluding to a covenant between God and Abraham which is plainly bilateral, involving not only divine promises but also human obligations, and which is perpetuated from one generation to the next through the rite of circumcision."[15]

Thus, the seal of "forever" signing the clause of Israelites' obligations to circumcision was an important part of P's holistic picture of the covenant. Westermann argues that circumcision was a rite[16] that

---

to walk before God and be perfect" (G. J. Wenham, *Genesis 16-50* <Dallas: Word Books, 1994>, p. 31.
[15] Williamson, *Abraham, Israel and the Nations*, p. 150.
[16] Hamilton writes: "Circumcision does not identify Israelites *qua* Israelites to non-Israelites, for many non-Israelites already practiced the same rite" (Hamilton, *The Book of Genesis, Chapters 1-17* <Grand Rapids: Eerdmans, 1990>, p. 470). But it is important to note that the real significance of the ritual of circumcision for the Israelites was internal group identity. In other words, circumcision was important for how Israelites viewed themselves as a people (of the covenant) and as individuals (in the covenant). Circumcision was not intended to "show off" Israelite identity to others. Thus, efforts to place circumcision as a physical, outward show to others of Israelite identity are not necessary. Michael V. Fox writes: "There is no point in referring the custom to a time when people went naked, for that custom is certainly not relevant for P, and even in the earliest times Israelites did not go naked" (Michael V. Fox, "The Sign of the Covenant: Circumcision in the Light of the

lies outside the cult and originally had no connection to worshipping God, but the Exile prompted the change. P innovated and elevated circumcision to the status of covenantal obligation as a sign of belonging to the people of Yahweh. In other words, it was intended to be an ethnic identity marker raised to the status of cultic ritual and observance.[17] It is hard to determine based on available material evidence if circumcision did not exist as a cultic practice before the Exile. However, it is important to note that it was perceived as a cultic practice certainly by the writing of P in the Exile. This means that the ritual of circumcision, understood to be tied to cultic ritual, acted in synecdotal relationship, whereby a part of the cultic system was held up as crucial for existence of Israelites as a people of Yahweh. In other words, circumcision in the context of Genesis 17 functioned to emphasize all cultic rituals. Van Seters writes: "The cultic institution of circumcision ... corresponds so completely with the whole style and orientation of the priestly code...."[18] P outlined importance of cultic observance in the covenantal formula in the simplest way possible. And "forever" signed the legal obligation of Israelites to observe cultic ritual.

In fact, "forever" was used as a covenantal seal by P to sign each clause of the covenant and it was purposely meant to be didactic and explanatory in the context of the Exile. And this covenantal seal

---

Priestly *'ôt* Etiologies," *Revue biblique* <81 (1974), pp. 557-596>, p. 595).
[17] Westermann, *Genesis 12-36*, 264.
[18] Van Seters, *Abraham in History and Tradition,* 281.

can be seen as a purposeful and deliberate seal on the part of P. This becomes clear when one compares the covenant account in Genesis 15. Genesis 15 is missing the covenantal seal of "forever." This can be understood by the fact that Genesis 15 is attributable to JE[19] and is often seen by in large as pre-Exile in composition. It was a period when there was no need to doubt the covenant with God. Israelites were in the land of the covenant and cultic worship of God was in session. There was not the despondency of the Exile, where Israelites were displaced from the land of Israel. Genesis 15 points to a background in which there was no explicit need to remind people of the promises of God; Israelites were experiencing the covenantal blessings in every day life.

---

[19] Various scholars have posited their own theories of how J and E sources formed the composite nature of JE in Genesis 15. J. Wellhausen argues that Genesis 15:1-6 is E and Genesis 15:7-21 is J (J. Wellhausen, *Die Komposition des Hexateuchs und der historischen Bücher des Alten Testaments* <Berlin: W. de Gruyter, 1963>, pp. 21-22). H. Gunkel argues for a greater integration of J and E sources in the text. Gunkel posits that verses 1b, 3a, 5, 11, 12a, 13a, 14, and 16 belong to E and the rest belong J (H. Gunkel, *Genesis*, trans. M. Biddle <Macon: Mercer University Press, 1997>, pp. 176-177). N. Lohfink argues that J almost entirely reworked E in Genesis 15 <Stuttgart: Katholisches Bibelwerk, 1967>, pp. 35-44). It is important to note that in a computer assisted research revealed that there was no real difference in the styles of J and E, indicating a potential unified origin of J and E. See Y. T. Radday and H. Shore, *Genesis: An Authorship Study in Computer-Assisted Statistical Linguistics* (Rome: Biblical Institute Press, 1985).

Some scholars have even commented that Genesis 15 represents a promise[20] of God and pictures a unilateral covenant. In other words, obligations of Israelites are not mentioned; God would bless Israelites regardless of what Israelites will do. Such an opinion by scholars highlights the fact that Genesis 15 seems to be secure in the assurance that God blesses. This is completely understandable in Sitz im Leben of pre-Exile when Israelites were enjoying the covenantal blessings of God in the land of Israel. There was no need to question God's promises or blessings because it was a part of everyday life. It is during the time of the Exile that questions about God's promises were asked. Particularly because displaced Israelites had already tasted the covenantal blessing in the land of Israel, it was difficult for Israelites to accept that God could be faithful in the covenant. Genesis 17 represents such a period and answers the questions. Genesis 17, therefore, emphasizes Israelites' covenantal obligations of circumcision as an everlasting covenant. The understanding is that the Exile happened because Israelites violated their clause in the everlasting covenant. Westermann notes that the covenant of God with Abraham as outlined in Genesis 17 represents a covenant of God with Israel and it "obviously establishes a lasting situation which binds ... in a mutual obligation."[21] Thus, there was hope because

---

[20] John Skinner simply assumes that the covenant is a promise and uses the word "promise" throughout in his commentary (John Skinner, *A Critical and Exegetical Commentary* <Edinburgh: T. & T. Clark, 1930>, pp. 276-280).

[21] Westermann, *Genesis 12-36*, 113.

the covenant was everlasting, so the promises of God could be restored when Israelites resumed keeping their part of the covenant. That is the message of P in Genesis 17. The difference between the covenant passages of JE and P can be understood in light of their Sitz im Leben.

I would actually argue that Genesis 15 was not a unilateral promise on God's part. It is because of its Sitz im Leben that the responsibility of the Israelites are played down whereas Genesis 17 emphasizes Israelite responsibility and makes it an integral part of the covenant formula. My argument that Genesis 15 emphasizes bilateral agreement is based primarily on a ritual of the covenant. Genesis 15:10 accounts Abraham bringing animals requested by God and cutting them in half. This is a ritual to say that Abraham and his descendants are bound to their part in the covenant. God testifies to his obligations by passing through the cut pieces. Nahum M. Sarna writes: "It is generally believed that when the contracting parties passed between the several pieces they thereby accepted the covenant obligations and invoked upon themselves the fate of the animals if the terms of the pact were violated."[22] There is thus an implicit understanding that the covenant is made between two parties and both parties are obligated to the covenant. If one party breaks the covenant, then the other party is no longer obliged to keep their part of the covenant.

In this sense, Genesis 15 and Genesis 17 are similar. Both are bilateral agreements which obligate

---

[22] Nahum M. Sarna, *Understanding Genesis* (New York: McGraw-Hill Book Company, 1966), p. 126.

two parties to keeping their part of the covenant. In both passages, it is understood that if one party breaks their covenant obligation, then the other party is not obliged to keep their part. Genesis 17 makes this point more explicitly. Furthermore, both Genesis 15 and Genesis 17 are similar in emphasizing the concept of the everlasting nature of the covenant. Genesis 15 does not utilize the covenant seal phrase of "forever," but the idea is there. Promise made to Abraham would continue through his descendants. Abraham seals the covenant on behalf of himself and his descendants.

There are several reasons why Genesis 17 has the covenant seal of "forever" whereas Genesis 15 does not. As mentioned before, it relates to the Sitz im Leben[23] of the composition and the needs of the community at the time. There was a practical need in the Exile, which is represented in the voice of Genesis 17, to emphasize that the covenant was forever. The covenantal seal of "forever" served this purpose. However, there are other reasons as well.

---

[23] R. W. L. Moberly argues that the Patriarchal material is non-Israelite and that Israelite religion began with Moses (R. W. L. Moberly, *Genesis 12-50* <Sheffield: JSOT Press, 1992>, 15). Moberly's ideas are helpful for understanding the diachronic development of Patriarchal materials as redacted and retold by later composers, such as JE and P. Even if one argues that Patriarchal materials existed hundreds of years before JE and P, one cannot deny that it is difficult to see Patriarchal materials apart from the background of JE and P. They had their own agenda and were products of their historical experiences. In other words, JE and P's account of the Patriarchs describes more about them and their setting than about the Patriarchs.

Genesis 17 is a more developed document[24] than Genesis 15 from a legal perspective. McEvenue writes regarding P's work of Genesis 17: "Clearly he has drawn his materials from pentateuchal sources: he has taken the formal and yet plastic narrative of Gen 15, and the delightful family tale of Gen 18, 1-6, and turned the oath of the one and the promise of the other into a very solemn legal-theological statement."[25] Indeed, there is a clear difference in style. Scholars, such as Westermann, have mentioned that Genesis 17 is less like a narrative,[26] which Genesis 15 is, and more like a speech of God. Although it takes the form of a speech of God, it is more like a coherent legal document with clauses indicating clear obligations. The covenantal seal of "forever" is a part of development in legal language. It marks each clause of the covenant. Thus, one can see Genesis 17 as a diachronic development in terms of the drafting of the covenant from Genesis 15.[27] In other words,

---

[24] McEvenue argues that P is entirely dependent on JE (McEvenue, *The Narrative Style of the Priestly Writer*, 181-182). Thus, for McEvenue, Genesis 17 represents pure linear development from Genesis 15 and related JE sources.

[25] McEvenue, *The Narrative Style of the Priestly Writer*, 145-146.

[26] Westermann, *Genesis 12-36*, 254.

[27] This is the scholarly consensus. However, there are some who disagree with the diachronic approach. Williamson argues that Genesis 15 and Genesis 17 represent two separate covenants (Williamson, *Abraham, Israel and the Nations*, pp. 78-120). For disagreement with the diachronic approach, also see B. Jacob, *Das erste Buch der Tora: Genesis übersetzt und erklärt* (Berlin: Schocken Books, 1934) and S. R. Külling, *Zur Datierung der "Genesis-P-Stücke": Namentlich des Kapitels Genesis 17* (Kampen: Kok, 1964). Furthermore, see T. D.

although Genesis 15 and Genesis 17 are pointing to the same covenant, Genesis 17 is more specific and legalistic in language because it represents a type of conscious revision of Genesis 15. Some scholars have tried to explain advanced legal status of the covenant in the language of the covenant in Genesis 17 in terms of institutions. Westermann writes regarding Genesis 17: "Here something is 'set up,' founded and established, and 'between me and you'; something between God and Abraham's descendants that is to last through generations; it is to last for ever לברית עולם. This is a really classical description of an institution."[28] Thirdly, and not unrelated to first two points, the covenant seal of "forever" in Genesis 17 is a key signifier. In other words, the term "forever" is used intentionally and consciously as a term to spur community to action by associating with the word the mythic traditions associated with the concept. In other words, "forever" served a key literary function as a literary tool to prompt action. Westermann writes: "This priestly theologian was conscious that he was bound to traditions which were not merely at his disposal in literary form, but which he also acknowledged and wanted to preserve as a part of living tradition."[29] Although Genesis 17 is a legal document, it was primarily intended to be read or heard by the Israelite community. The covenantal seal of "forever," therefore, became a key signifier in its literary function as a type of rallying call.

Alexander's Ph.D. thesis, *A Literary Analysis of the Abraham Narrative in Genesis* (The Queen's University of Belfast, 1982).
[28] Westermann, *Genesis 12-36*, 262.
[29] Westermann, *Genesis 12-36*, 256.

The word "forever" came to take on symbolic significance precisely because of its link to the covenant. As a covenantal seal, "forever" functioned as a key signifier for generations following P. To a certain extent, the fact that "forever" gained a historic force of foundational stories tied later generations to the term and to the covenant that employed the term in important ways. J. P. Fokkelman writes:

> The stories about the patriarchs, which in ancient Israel no doubt functioned as authoritative texts (their canonization is by no means accidenttal) on the national history, are evidence of an elementary urge to occupy one's mind with one's own history. That these sagas as religious texts are samples of a most specific interpretation detracts nothing from the basic fact so characteristic of ancient Israel: viz. that in its own opinion, it is both here and often elsewhere busy verbalizing its own history, transforming it in a religiously authorized way, inventing it, and repeating it.[30]

Thus, in the form of reinvention and authoritative transformation as we have the covenant in Genesis 17, עולם functioned as a covenant seal with the literary and ideological imprint of P and the Sitz im Leben of

---

[30] J. P. Fokkelman, *Narrative Art in Genesis: Specimens of Stylistic and Structural Analysis* (Assen: Van Gorcum, 1975), 239.

the Exile. And this legal document exerted cultic and social influence well into the Second Temple period.

Bibliography

Fokkelman, J. P. *Narrative Art in Genesis: Specimens of Stylistic and Structural Analysis.* Assen: Van Gorcum, 1975.

Fox, Michael V. "The Sign of the Covenant: Circumcision in the Light of the Priestly *'ôt* Etiologies." *Revue biblique* 81 (1974), pp. 557-596.

Gunkel, H. *Genesis.* Translated by M. Biddle. Macon: Mercer University Press, 1997.

Hamilton, V. P. *The Book of Genesis 1-17.* Grand Rapids: Eerdmans, 1990.

Jacob, B. *Das erste Buch der Tora: Genesis übersetzt und erklärt.* Berlin: Schocken Books, 1934.

Külling, S. R. *Zur Datierung der "Genesis-P-Stücke": Nomentlich des Kapitels Genesis 17.* Kampen: Kok, 1964.

Lohfink, N. *Die Landverheissung als Eid: Eine Studie zu Gn 15.* Stuttgart: Katholisches Bibelwerk, 1967.

McEvenue, Sean E. *The Narrative Style of the Priestly Writer.* Rome: Biblical Institute Press, 1971.

Millard, A. R., and D. J. Wiseman (Editors). *Essays on the Patriarchal Narratives.* Winona Lake: Eisenbrauns, 1983.

Moberly, R. W. L. *Genesis 12-50.* Sheffield: JSOT Press, 1992.

Radday, Y. T., and H. Shore. *Genesis: An Authorship Study in Computer-Assisted Statistical Linguistics.* Rome: Biblical Institute Press, 1985.

Sailhamer, J. H. *The Pentateuch as Narrative: A Biblical-Theological Commentary.* Grand Rapids: Zondervan, 1992.

Sarna, Nahum M. *Understanding Genesis.* New York: McGraw-Hill Book Company, 1966.

Skinner, John. *A Critical and Exegetical Commentary on Genesis.* Edinburgh: T. & T. Clark, 1930.

Thompson, Thomas L. *The Origin Tradition of Ancient Israel: The Literary Formation of Genesis and Exodus 1-23.* Sheffield: Sheffield Academic Press, 1987.

Van Seters, John. *Abraham in History and Tradition*. New Haven: Yale University Press, 1975.

Von Rad, Gerhard. *Genesis: A Commentary*. Translated by John H. Marks. London: SCM Press Ltd., 1961.

Wellhausen, J. *Die Komposition des Hexateuchs und der historischen Bücher des Alten Testaments*. Berlin: W. de Gruyter, 1963.

Wenham, G. J. *Genesis 16-50*. Dallas: Word Books, 1994.

Westermann, Claus. *Genesis 12-36: A Commentary*. Translated by John J. Scullion. Minneapolis: Augsburg Publishing House, 1985.

Williamson, Paul R. *Abraham, Israel and the Nations: The Patriarchal Promise and its Covenantal Development in Genesis*. Sheffield: Sheffield Academic Press, 2000.

"Nuzi, Women's Rights, and Hurrian Ethnicity: Land Ownership and Adoption of Women as a Key to Unlocking the Past"[1]

The discovery[2] at Nuzi had a profound impact in the study of the ancient Near East. Among the

---

[1] I would like to thank Professor Tammi Schneider of Claremont Graduate University for reading the complete draft of the paper and offering helpful comments.

[2] The story behind the discovery of Nuzi is interesting. It was a co-operative working alliance made between the government of Iraq and newly opened (in 1923) American School of Oriental Research (ASOR) in Baghdad. Professor Edward Chiera of the University of Pennsylvania was the Annual Professor and Professor in Charge of ASOR in Iraq in 1924-1925. During his stay in Iraq, Miss Gertrude Bell was the Honorary Director of the Department of Antiquities of the Iraqi government. Miss Bell on behalf of the Iraqi government asked Professor Chiera to undertake an excavation near Kirkuk where cuneiform tablets were found by the native Iraqis. In 1925, Professor Chiera began the excavation of Yalghan Tappa which resulted in an excavation of the mansion of a Hurrian magnate (after a few months of excavation) and the discovery of Nuzi (George A. Barton, "The Baghdad School," *The Annual of the American Schools of Oriental Research. Vol. VI for 1924-1925* <New Haven: Yale University Press, 1926, pp. 10-12>, p. 11). The Iraqi government was so pleased with their alliance and over the thousands of ancient doments discovered at Nuzi that it invited (following the suggestion of Gertrude Bell) ASOR in Baghdad to be housed in the new building of the Baghdad Museum (Barton, p. 12). But in 1927, Harvard University replaced the Iraqi Museum as the joint sponsor of the Nuzi excavations. And subsequent discoveries came to be housed in the Harvard Semitic Museum (Millar Burrows and E. A. Speiser, *The Annual of the American Schools of Oriental Research. Vol. XVI.* <New

most significant of the Nuzi discoveries is insight into the status of women in the ancient Near East in the second millennium BC. Surprisingly, women possessed tremendous social, economic, and personal power. The Nuzi archive indicates a social environment in which women enjoyed significant rights, such as the right to own property and engage in commerce. In fact, the social institution of adoption of women attests to the favorable treatment of women at Nuzi. I would argue that the enjoyment of such great rights in the context of the ancient world was possible because of the historical experience of Hurrians as an ethnic people in Nuzi.

For a society almost two millennia before the birth of Jesus of Nazareth, it is remarkable to see the extent to which women enjoyed rights. Women at Nuzi enjoyed rights to own[3] private property[4] and

---

Haven: American Schools of Oriental Research, 1936>, p. 5). In 1928-1929, Professor R. H. Pfeiffer as Director of ASOR in Baghdad began to excavate with the purpose of discovering what was under the Hurrian city of Nuzi. After sinking a shaft in the room (L4) in the mansion area, two tablets of the Agade period were discovered. In 1930-1931, Director R. F. S. Starr continued excavating the site and discovered over 200 tablets. Among the discoveries was a map, considered to be the oldest map in existence today (Theophile James Meek, "Some Gleanings from the Last Excavations at Nuzi," *The Annual of the American Schools of Oriental Research. Vol. XIII for 1931-1932* <New Haven: Yale University Press, 1933, pp. 1-12>, p. 1).

[3] Jack Goody and S. J. Tambiah write: "It must be clear that the question whether or not land was a woman's portion, either as a dowry or as inheritance, is of fundamental importance for other aspects of the social system" (Jack Goody and S. J. Tambiah, *Bridewealth and Dowry* <Cambridge: University Press, 1973>, p. 21).

engage in commerce.[5] Such rights of women are attested in tablets found at Nuzi describing the

---

[4] Babylonians were against women owning land. The Code of Hammurabi distinguished between two types of land possession: (1) *ilku* possessions and (2) private possessions. *Ilku* possession was land granted by the king as a reward for public services and could not be sold seized, mortgaged or passed down except to the male heir only on the condition of fulfilment of duties. Daughters could not inherit *ilku* possessions. The other type of land property in Babylonian custom was private property. Private property could be passed on to women. However, women were entitled only to the usufruct of the land and not to a real ownership of it (L. Delaporte, *Mesopotamia: The Babylonian and Assyrian Civilization*, trans. V. Gordon Childe <London: Kegan Paul, Trench, Trubner & Co. Ltd., 1925>, p. 101). Whereas men could sell property, women could not. An example of this common Babylonian custom is found in the lady Silim-Ishtar in the thirty-fifth year of Nebuchadrezzar II who retained the usufruct of her property. On her death, it passed on to her only daughter as she had no male child. Gula-qâ'ishat, the daughter, could not sell the land without her husband's authorization (Delaporte, p. 85). In essence, it was supposed that the daughter inherited only the usufruct of the land and technically the real ownership belonged to the daughter's husband, who was a man although no direct descendant of the mother. This shows the prohibition against women's real ownership of land in Babylonian tradition.

[5] The right for women to engage in commerce existed in the Babylonian society. For instance, when a woman's husband was off to war and she had no adult son, the wife managed the estate and a third of the estate from commerce was given to her personally (Delaporte, p. 76). However, this should be seen more as a right granted as the result of necessity rather than a normative right. In fact, Babylonian husbands could reduce their wives to servitude. Although Hammurabi reduced the maximum term of enslaving one's wife to three years, he did not destroy the institution. It was not uncommon in Babylon for a husband to sell his unfaithful wife into slavery (Delaporte, p. 76).

women of king's household. There were three types of women in the king's household: *sal.lugal*, *esrītu* women, and *mārāti šarri*.

Sal.lugal is translated "queen" and is seen to be the chief wife of the king (or in some cases, highly regarded secondary wife). They were entrepreneurs who owned land and engaged in business. *Esrītu* women were concubines of the king. The term is found only during this time in Assyria, the Hittite lands, and Mitanni and may be distinctively Hurrian in nature. The *esrītu* women owned property and engaged in business. They also held a high status in the community. *Mārāti šarri* were daughters of the king. They were often landowners with households. The high status of women in Nuzi is attested by the fact that the daughters of the king[6] inherited[7] along

---

[6] When looking at Nuzi, it is important to take A. Leo Oppenheim's statement seriously. Oppenheim writes: "A primary characteristic of Mesopotamian societal structure appears to have been the absence of any non-economic status stratification, if one disregards the unique status of the king and excludes the slave population that was at all times rather small and in private hands. This statement will doubless have to be qualified somewhat for specific regions and periods where alien influences are in evidence" (A. Leo Oppenheim, *Ancient Mesopotamia: Portrait of a Dead Civilization* <Chicago: The University of Chicago Press, 1964>, p. 74). Nuzi represented foreign Hurrian influence.

[7] In ancient Babylonia (as seen in the Code of Hammurabi), sons generally inherited land. If land inheritance was extended to the daughter, it was understood that she did not own the property but rather she enjoyed the property which her brothers acted as trustees for. When she died, the land ownership was transferred to her brothers in full (C. H. W. Johns, *Babylonian and Assyrian Laws, Contracts and Letters* <New York: Charles Scribner's Sons, 1904>, p. 161). A. Leo Oppenheim recognizes

with the sons of the king (*mārē šarri*) according to rank.[8]

It is important to note that a woman's right to inherit her father's property was not confined to royalty; rather, it was the normative practice at Nuzi. The division of father's property happened after the death of the father. The chief heir received a double portion of the property while other sons received a single share. Along with the sons, unmarried daughters received their portion of the father's land as inheritance. Those women who married while their father was alive received a dowry so they, in effect, received their inheritance in advance. Women's right to inherit was so important at Nuzi that it was assumed that the woman was an heir to inherit a portion. Katarzyna Grosz writes:

> In a majority of Nuzi testaments no provisions are made for daughters. In some cases one could assume that the testators had no daughters at all, but the probability is that in at least fifty percent of all cases the daughters were already provided for, i.e. married at the moment when the will was written. If this was not the case, i.e. if the testator still had an unmarried daughter at the

---

that Nuzi represented an example of foreign influence on typical Babylonian family (Oppenheim, p. 77).

[8] Florence Morgan Gillman, "Nuzi," *The Anchor Bible Dictionary Volume 4 K-N*, ed. David Noel Freedman, Gary A. Herion, David F. Graf, and John David Pleins (New York: Doubleday, 1992, pp. 1156-1162).

moment of the writing of the will, she was treated as an heir and received her share.[9]

Women's right to own property was attached to her right to engage in commerce as agriculture was the main source of trade and income.[10]

Besides the fact that women could own property and engage in commerce, adoption of women at Nuzi attests to high regard for women. Ṭuppi mārtūti was the most common adoption of women and clearly shows high regard for women and women's rights. This type of adoption[11] was generally concluded by parties who were familiar to each other before the adoption transaction[12] and clearly shows upholding the interest of the adopted girl. The

---

[9] Katarzyna Grosz, "Dowry and Brideprice in Nuzi," *Studies on the Civilization and Culture of Nuzi and the Hurrians: In Honor of Ernest R. Lacheman on his Seventy-Fifth Birthday April 29, 1981*, ed. M. A. Morrison and D. I. Owen (Winona Lake: Eisenbrauns, 1981, pp. 161-182), p. 165.

[10] Grosz, "Dowry and Brideprice in Nuzi," p. 164.

[11] Other types of adoption (*ṭuppi kallatūti* and *ṭuppi mārtūti u kallatūti*) did not necessarily involve parties who knew each other. However, general principles of *ṭuppi mārtūti* operated; that is, there was a clause requiring the adopted girl's marriage. Underlying all types of adoption of women was the concern for the adopted girl's present and future well-being including her marriage and formation of a family. In terms of the structure of the contract of adopting women, all types of adoption shared the same format and same kind of obligations (Grosz, "On Some Aspects of Adoption of Women at Nuzi," pp. 143-147).

[12] Katarzyna Grosz, "On Some Aspects of the Adoption of Women at Nuzi," *Studies on the Civilization and Culture of Nuzi and the Hurrians (Volume 2)*, ed. D. I. Owen and M. A. Morrison (Winona Lake: Eisenbrauns, 1987), p. 139.

adoptant was expected to educate the adopted girl and equip her socially besides the obligation of feeding and clothing her. Furthermore, almost all *mārtūtu* transactions explicitly contained clauses regarding the future marriage of the girl. The adoption, therefore, was for the girl's explicit well-being.[13]

Thus, Katarzyna Grosz describes the adoption of women as a kind of godparentage.[14] The adopted girl remained a daughter to her natural parents while gaining additional parents. In fact, Grosz allows for the possibility that the adopted girl was being allowed to remain physically in her natural parents' household. Like godparentage, the adoptant gave the adopted girl greater prestige as the adoptant tended to be of high social status.

But it is important to note that the adoption was not symbolic but actual. In this regard, Grosz's alternative way of describing *ṭuppi mārtūti* as a relationship between a patron and a client[15] may be more helpful. The adopting patron was to provide the girl with life-long support. Arranging for a sound marriage was a part of this patron-obligation. In other words, the institution of the adoption of women was to advance the adopted girl's interest in society.

This is evident even further when we look at the "gift" of adoption. The adoptant paid the parents

---

[13] Grosz, "On Some Aspects of the Adoption of Women at Nuzi," p. 133.
[14] Grosz, "On Some Aspects of the Adoption of Women at Nuzi," p. 140.
[15] Grosz, "On Some Aspects of the Adoption of Women at Nuzi," p. 141.

or individuals who gave the girl up for adoption a sum of money as a gift. On account of the exchange of money, it may seem like the adopted girl's interest was not primary. However, when we look at the amount of money exchanged, it puts everything in perspective. Their adoptant gave the parents giving the girl up for adoption the amount between ten and twenty-five shekels of silver. This amount is far below the amount of money paid to a woman's parents/family when a woman is taken in marriage, which was forty-five shekels of silver.[16] Thus, the girl's parents lost a large sum of money in giving her away before her marriage. But the adoptant did not profit either since the girl was adopted at a young age and had to be housed, clothed, educated, and given a respectable marriage. Even if the adoptant received forty shekels of silver at the adopted girl's marriage, the difference (or "profit") of fifteen to thirty shekels of silver did not come close to money spent on the adopted girl's rearing process. Furthermore, it was possible for the girl to die before marriage, which meant that the adoptant would receive nothing, since marriage price was paid at marriage. In this case, the adoptant would have been out ten to twenty-five pieces of silver paid for adopting her and costs incurred for housing, feeding, and rearing the adopted child. Clearly, the *ṭuppi mārtūti* adoption of women at Nuzi was for the interests of the women adopted.

The concern for the adopted woman is also clear from the stipulations regarding to whom the adoptant is allowed to marry her off. In Katarzyna

---

[16] Grosz, "On Some Aspects of the Adoption of Women at Nuzi," p. 133.

Grosz's study, out of twenty-eight *mārtūtu* transactions, all except four tablets explicitly prohibit marriage to a slave. In fact, some adoption transactions specifically emphasize the adoptant's obligation to marry the adopted daughter to the adoptant's son, an adopted son, or a free man.[17] Such a stipulation, in fact, had the result of making the adopted daughter an integral part of the adoptant's household. Even after the marriage, the adopted woman would remain in the household because she would be likely to marry the adoptant's natural son or an adopted son. The clause allowing for marriage to a freeman should be seen as an "out" clause. The expectation, of course, is that if the adoptant chooses to marry the adopted daughter off to a freeman that he would be of similar status as the adoptant's son.

The case of the adopted son is significant as well because the adopted son inherited property and was seen as an integral part of the household.[18] Furthermore, often wealthier and more influential members of society got themselves adopted in order to inherit property of petty landowners.[19] Thus, it

---

[17] Grosz, "On Some Aspects of the Adoption of Women at Nuzi," pp. 137-138.

[18] General Babylonian perception of adoption was for the sake of perpetuating the family for barren couples, who have abandoned hope of having any more children (Delaporte, p. 79). At Nuzi, it was far more than that.

[19] Land sale was prohibited at Nuzi and adoption was a way around it (Edward Chiera and Ephraim Speiser, "A New Factor in the History of the Ancient Near East," *The Annals of the American Schools of Oriental Research. Vol. VI for 1924-1925*, ed. Benjamin W. Bacon <New Haven: Yale University Press, 1926, pp. 75-92>, p. 86). In contrast, land sale was generally allowed in Babylonia (Johns, p. 184).

was conceivable that adopted son may be of higher economic and social status than the adoptant. Certainly, *ṭuppi mārtūti* transactions intended to advance the social standing of the adopted girl.

Even the four tablets which allowed for the adoptant to marry the adopted girl to whomever he/she wishes[20] should be seen as positively reflecting on supporting the adopted woman's interest. This would be the case even if the adoptant married the adopted woman to a slave.[21] The fact was that slaves (*wardus*) at Nuzi could own property and engage in a variety of contracts, such as land acquisition and adoption. In fact, some slaves were far wealthier and held property much more than an average freeman at Nuzi. Pai-Tešup, the slave of Prince Šilwa-Tešup, is a good example.[22] The benefits of marrying a slave at ancient Nuzi is described effectively by Grosz:

---

[20] Grosz, "On Some Aspects of the Adoption of Women at Nuzi," p. 137.

[21] The situation for slaves in Babylonia was generally very good. Johns writes: "But the slave had a great amount of freedom, and was in no respect worse off than a child or even a wife [of the slave owner]" (Johns, p. 168). In fact, the status of slaves at Nuzi is in line with that of slaves generally in Babylonia. This is not surprising given the fact that Hurrians transmitted Babylonian culture. Joan Oates emphasizes the point: "Perhaps the most important role of the Hurrians in the story of Babylon lies in the part they played as intermediaries in the transmission of Babylonian culture to the Hittites, to the Palestinians and Phoenicians, and, indirectly, to Greece and the western world" (Joan Oates, *Babylon* <London: Thames and Hudson, 1979>, p. 87). However, it is important to recognize that there were differences despite the similarity.

[22] Gillman, pp. 1157-1158.

> What was the position of a free-born woman married to a slave, and which parent would envisage the possibility of marrying his daughter to a slave? In replying to these questions two facts must be stressed: 1) the economic situation of some poor but free-born persons could be considerably improved by marriage to a wealthy slave, and 2) in a society where even a free person could envisage enslavement in certain situations (e.g., debt, capture in war or by slavers, or punishment for certain offenses), distinctions between free and slave must not have been so clear-cut....[23]

Thus, even when the marriage clause in the adoption agreement allowed for a marriage to a slave, it can be understood to be in the adopted woman's best interest.

Enjoyment of rights by women and favorable treatment of women were possible at Nuzi because of the historical experience of Hurrians as an ethnic people at Nuzi. Nuzi was the new name given to the city of Gasur, near Kirkuk, after Hurrians occupied it. The Hurrians were a non-Semitic people unlike the population they occupied. So who were the Hurrians?

The origin of Hurrians is not clear. A part of the reason for this is due to the fact that unlike Hittites, Hurrians as a political group were dominant in Near Eastern politics for a relatively short period

---

[23] Grosz, "On Some Aspects of the Adoption of Women at Nuzi," p. 147.

of time, not playing a significant role until the middle of the second millennium BC.[24] Further complicating the problem is the fact that there is no word for "foreigner" in Mesopotamia from the Ur III period and "later periods of Mesopotamian history."[25] This is true of the Hurrians. They were, in fact, foreigners but were not called foreigners in any way. It was their personal name [26] which identified them as Hurrians. Texts generally do not identify Hurrians as foreigners explicitly but may indicate their foreign identity via inference by stating their origin from a certain city.[27] Since there is no focus on the foreign identity of Hurrians, there is no explicit discussion regarding their ethnic identity.

The language of the Hurrians[28] is helpful for understanding their origins and ethnic identity.

---

[24] Georges Roux, *Ancient Iraq* (London: George Allen & Unwin Ltd., 1964), p. 192.

[25] Giorgio Buccellati, *The Amorites of the Ur III Period* (Naples: Istituto Orientale di Napoli, 1966), p. 324.

[26] Michael C. Astour writes: "A name is considered Hurrian if it is composed of one or more elements that have no obvious Semitic etymology but are clearly attested in continuous Hurrian texts, or as Hurrianisms in Akkadian-written texts, or as Hurrian entries in ancient cuneiform vocabularies, or serve as elements characteristically Hurrian personal and geographical names" (Michael C. Astour, "Semites and Hurrians in Northern Transtigris," *Studies on the Civilization and Culture of Nuzi and the Hurrians. Volume 2*, ed. D. I. Owen and M. A. Morrison <Winona Lake: Eisenbrauns, 1987, pp. 3-68>, p. 3).

[27] Buccellati, pp. 324-325.

[28] Chiera and Speiser prefer to see Hurrian as a language group (Chiera and Speiser, p. 80). They, in fact, viewed Mitanni as a "dialect" of Hurrian (Chiera and Speiser, p. 79).

Georges Roux identifies Hurrian,[29] which is written in cuneiform script, as belonging to the "Asianic" language group and not to Semites or Indo-European language group. Hurrian's nearest language relative is Urartian, which is a language of Urarṭu (Armenia) in the first millennium BC. Based on this information, Roux identifies Armenia as the original homeland of the Hurrians.[30] In fact, the original excavator of Nuzi in 1925 who discovered the site, Professor Edward Chiera, identifies Hurrians of Nuzi as having originated in Armenia.[31]

Although Sumerians, and not Hurrians, were the original population of Mesopotamia, Hurrian tribes were present in areas of Mesopotamia as early as the third millennium. In the second millennium, the Hurrians helped establish a powerful Mitanni-Hurrian empire under the leadership of an Indo-European ruling class.[32] And the Hurrians spread wide and far. E. A. Speiser describes the extent of their reach: "Through our knowledge of Hurrian proper names we have arrived at the realization that the people in question were to be found, for the better part of the millennium, scattered all the way from Anatolia to Elam and from Armenia to Egypt, interspersed with other ethnic elements or settled in colonies of their own."[33] But despite their wide reach,

---

[29] Hurrians themselves called their language Hurrian (*hur-li-li*) as is attested 16 times in the Hurrian sections of the archives of Boghaz Kevi (Chiera and Speiser, p. 80).
[30] Roux, pp. 192-193.
[31] Chiera and Speiser, p. 78.
[32] Chiera and Speiser, p. 82.
[33] E. A. Speiser, "Ethnic Movements in the Near East in the Second Millennium B.C.: The Hurrians and their connections

there is a considerable amount of confusion as to their identity. A part of the reason is that Hurrians were reluctant to refer to themselves as Hurrians. Their identity as Hurrians is inferred from their names.

But this is not to say that Hurrian identity was not real. It was real and important. Hurrians were, in fact, characterized by their own culture, mores, and laws as indicated by thousands of documents discovered at Nuzi. Nuzi represents a later stage of the expansion of the Hurrians. Assyrian elements are found at Nuzi, but Assyrians seemed inferior to the population at Nuzi because they were found selling themselves into slavery to Hurrian magnates of Nuzi. Thus, Chiera and Speiser date Nuzi discoveries before the Assyrian rise to power in the mid-fifteenth century.[34]

The historical tension at Nuzi caught between Assyrian servitude to Hurrians and later Assyrian dominance in the region, in fact, provides a key to understanding the Hurrians and their practices, including extension of great rights to women. Hurrians were a nomadic people often moving from one place to another. They were aware of their difference and sought to blend in with the people among whom they settled. Even when they became dominant and occupied a region, the Hurrians were

---

with the Habiru and the Hyksos," *The Annual of the American Schools of Oriental Research. Vol. XIII for 1931-1932*, ed. Millar Burrows and E. A. Speiser (New Haven: Yale University Press, 1993, pp. 13-54), p. 16.

[34] Chiera and Speiser, pp. 84-85.

interested to in blending in with the people they occupied.³⁵

This was a way of survival especially in the case of occupation. In most cases the native population far outnumbered the occupying Hurrian population. This is understandable especially in places like Nuzi which was a Semitic area before being occupied by Hurrians, who were non-Semitic and had their origins from a far-away place.

It is certain based on archaeological and textual evidence that there were no Hurrians in Nuzi in the Agade period, at the time of Naram-Sin, when the whole of Arrapha was a part of Subartu. The site of Nuzi was inhabited but by non-Hurrians. And the name of the city was different; it was called Gasur. Speiser states emphatically: "The Hurrians did not settle in Arrapha until after the Old-Akkadian period...."³⁶ Speiser adds: "In short, large portions of Subartu possessed non-Hurrian population prior to the second millennium. The Hurrians were clearly new-comers who made their appearance at a comparatively late date."³⁷ Being new-comers, Hurrians undoubtedly possessed anxiety about the longevity of their settlement in a largely Semitic area. As

---

³⁵ Hurrians' success at blending in is attested by the fact that they are confused with Subareans. Speiser writes: "It is a fact that later Assyrian kings referred to the Hurrians by the newly coined term *šubarî*. But this did not take place until the Hurrians had been in the country for centuries. It is a not unusual instance of modifying an old native name for the purpose of applying it, in a specialized sense, to a new largely assimilated people" (Speiser, p. 25).
³⁶ Speiser, p. 24.
³⁷ Speiser, p. 25.

new-comers, Hurrians realized that they could not completely blend in even if they tried hard to. They were an ethnic unit.[38]

Besides this ethnic awareness along with the knowledge of their relative instability due to recent settlement and the demographics[39] of the region, the fact and history of their ethnic experience defined Nuzi practices, including extending great rights to women. Hurrians were wanderers. And they were wanderers since the third millennium BC. But they were not wanderers by choice, but rather by necessity for survival.[40] Because they were pushed into their wanderings in such a way, the Hurrians had anxiety about survival. All these factors, thus, contributed to the extending of rights to women.

---

[38] Speiser writes: "The Hurrians can always be recognized by their characteristic proper names: they were an ethnic unit" (Speiser, pp. 34-35).

[39] Besides the fact that the region of Nuzi was largely Semitic to begin with, there were other nomadic people, such as the Habiru who were largely Semitic in nature (Speiser, pp. 34-35). Furthermore, J. A. Brinkman notes that "detailed archival study and genealogical reconstruction trace the presence of one Kassite family in the Nuzi area over a period of seven generations and imply that this family may not have been atypical compared to other families dwelling in the same area: the Kassites may indeed have continued as a distinct and recognizable entity in a Hurrian milieu" (J. A. Brinkman, "Hurrians in Babylonia in the Late Second Millennium B.C.: An Unexploited Minority Resource for Socio-Economic and Philological Analysis," *Studies on the Civilization and Culture of Nuzi and the Hurrians: In Honor of Earnest R. Lacheman on his Seventy-Fifth Birthday April 29, 1981*, ed. M. A. Morrison and D. I. Owen <Winona Lake: Eisenbrauns, 1981, pp. 27-35>, p. 27).

[40] Speiser, p. 33.

Why should this be the case? The Hurrian numbers were few to start with, so extending greater power to Hurrian women would increase their numbers and, more importantly, the numbers of Hurrians holding power. Both male and female members of the Hurrian ethnic group would own land and be able to amass wealth through commerce, thereby making the Hurrian position at Nuzi more secure.

Like women's right to property ownership and commerce, the adoption of women should be seen in light of the Hurrian experience as an ethnic people in Nuzi. Hurrians were concerned that Hurrian girls were provided for and had secure marriages arranged so that the Hurrian position would be secure.[41] Having a marriage stipulation as an integral part of the adoption of woman secured Hurrian women's position – and by extension, Hurrian population's security – by law. Even if a Hurrian girl was adopted by a non-Hurrian wealthy individual, the adoptant would have been obligated by law to provide for the Hurrian girl and ensure her marriage and life security. It was important to protect Hurrian women and give them great rights to secure the Hurrian position at Nuzi.

The protection of women's rights and the expansion of it in Nuzi must be seen in the larger picture of Hurrian experience as an ethnic people

---

[41] Grosz writes: "If we perceive 'marriage adoptions' as economic transactions in which marrying rights to women are sold by their kinsmen, we shall fail to understand the role of these transactions in establishing important social ties within the Nuzi community" (Grosz, "On Some Aspects of the Adoption of Women at Nuzi," p. 152).

who settled in a largely Semitic area[42] with a resident insecurity about survival and an awareness of their ethnic identity. The prohibition to sell land, for instance, can be seen as a settled Hurrian population legislating to hinder sale of land by Hurrians who may face economic difficulties. The possibility of acquiring such land only thorugh adoption shows the Hurrian concern to provide for Hurrians who may need to give up their land. Even if they gave up their land through adoption, the Hurrians would not be pushed out of Nuzi. This provided anxious Hurrian population with security and a peace of mind.

Discoveries at Nuzi opened a door to understanding the Hurrians. By extension, it helped understanding of their practices guided by their historical experiences as a nomadic ethnic people of non-Semitic heritage who settled a largely Semitic area. The anxiety and practical needs of the Hurrians encouraged protecting women's rights and aggrandizing women's rights. This is evident in women's right to own land and to engage in commerce for profit-taking purposes. Furthermore, adoption of women at Nuzi indicates overarching concern for women's security and well-being. Hurrian women were vital in the equation for Hurrian survival. Due to the

---

[42] Even after the Hurrian "dominance" in the region, their presence seemed relatively negligible. Brinkman writes: "The Hurrians are only one among several ethno-linguistic groups who are present in significant numbers in Babylonia at this time, at least in the well-documented fourteenth and thirteenth centuries. Isolating the Hurrians is not a simple task methodologically, since there is no term corresponding to 'Hurrian' in the pertinent Babylonian documents and thus no person is ever labelled specifically as Hurrian" (Brinkman, p. 28).

forces of history, women at Nuzi enjoyed great rights. Discoveries at Nuzi is a very important factor in the study of women's rights and women's history.

Bibliography

Astour, Michael C. "Semites and Hurrians in Northern Transtigris." *Studies on the Civilization and Culture of Nuzi and the Hurrians. Volume 2.* Edited by D. I. Owen and M. A. Morrison. Winona Lake: Eisenbrauns, 1987. Pages 3-68.

Barton, George A. "The Baghdad School." *The Annual of the American Schools of Oriental Research. Vol. VI for 1924-1925.* Edited by Benjamin W. Bacon. New Haven: Yale University Press, 1926. Pages 10-12.

Brinkman, J. A. "Hurrians in Babylonia in the Late Second Millennium B.C.: An Unexploited Minority Resouce for Socio-Economic and Philological Analysis." *Studies on the Civilization and Culture of Nuzi and the Hurrians: In Honor of Ernest R. Lacheman on his Seventy-Fifth Birthday April 29, 1981.* Edited by M. A. Morrison and D. I. Owen. Winona Lake: Eisenbrauns, 1981. Pages 27-35.

Buccellati, Giorgio. *The Amorites of the Ur III Period.* Naples: Istituto Orientale di Napoli, 1966.

Burrows, Millar, and E. A. Speiser (Ed.). *The Annual of the American Schools of Oriental Research.*

Vol. XVI. New Haven: American Schools of Oriental Research, 1936.

Chiera, Edward, and Ephraim A. Speiser. "A New Factor in the History of the Ancient Near East." *The Annual of the American Schools of Oriental Research. Vol. VI for 1924-1925.* Edited by Benjamin W. Bacon. New Haven: Yale University Press, 1926. Pages 75-92.

Delaporte, L. *Mesopotamia: The Babylonian and Assyrian Civilization.* Translated by V. Gordon Childe. London: Kegan Paul, Trench, Trubner & Co. Ltd., 1925.

Gillman, Florence Morgan. "Nuzi." *The Anchor Bible Dictionary Volume 4 K-N.* Edited by David Noel Freedman, Gary A. Herion, David F. Graf, and John David Pleins. New York: Doubleday, 1992. Pages 1156-1162.

Goody, Jack, and S. J. Tambiah. *Bridewealth and Dowry.* Cambridge: University Press, 1973.

Grosz, Katarzyna. "Dowry and Brideprice in Nuzi." *Studies on the Civilization and Culture of Nuzi and the Hurrians: In Honor of Ernest R. Lacheman on his Seventy-Fifth Birthday April 29, 1981.* Edited by M. A. Morrison and D. I. Owen. Winona Lake: Eisenbrauns, 1981. Pages 161-182.

Grosz, Katarzyna. "On Some Aspects of the Adoption of Women at Nuzi." *Studies on the Civilization and Culture of Nuzi and the Hurrians. Volume 2.* Edited by D. I. Owen and M. A. Morrison. Winona Lake: Eisenbrauns, 1987.

Johns, C. H. W. *Babylonian and Assyrian Laws, Contracts and Letters.* New York: Charles Scribner's Sons, 1904.

Mayer, Walter. *Nuzi-Studien I: Die Archive des Palastes und die Prosopographie der Berufe.* Kevelaer: Verlag Butzon & Bercker, 1978.

Meek, Thophile James. "Some Gleanings from the Last Excavations at Nuzi." *The Annual of the American Schools of Oriental Research. Vol. XIII for 1931-1932.* Edited by Millar Burrows and E. A. Speiser. New Haven: Yale University Press, 1933. Pages 1-12.

Oates, Joan. *Babylon.* London: Thames and Hudson, 1979.

Oppenheim, A. Leo. *Ancient Mesopotamia: Portrait of a Dead Civilization.* Chicago: The University of Chicago Press, 1964.

Roux, Georges. *Ancient Iraq.* London: George Allen & Unwin Ltd., 1964.

Saggs, H. W. F. *Everyday Life in Babylonia & Assyria*. New York: Dorset Press, 1965.

Speiser, E. A. "Ethnic Movements in the Near East in the Second Millennium B.C.: The Hurrians and their Connections with the Habiru and the Hyksos." *The Annual of the American Schools of Oriental Research. Vol. XIII for 1931-1932.* Edited by Millar Burrows and E. A. Speiser. New Haven: Yale University Press, 1933. Pages 13-54.

Heerak Christian Kim

"Augustus' Manipulation of Traditional Roman Religion"[1]

Many sources from the ancient times describe Augustus as the restorer of order. Augustus ended civil strife and brought back emphasis on different aspects of traditional Roman religion. Thus, historians credit Augustus as having revived traditional Roman religion. Yet, upon careful examination of the nature of Roman religion and Augustus, one becomes sceptical of the word "revival" to describe Augustus' actions. Rather, it is more appropriate to describe Augustus as having manipulated Roman religions for his own political purposes.

There is much praise for Augustus from his contemporaries. The Provincial Assembly of Asia made a decree in 9 B.C. to worship Augustus as a god because he restored peace. First, Paulus Fabius Maximus put forth the proposal:

> [It is difficult to say] whether the birthday of the most divine Caesar has brought more of joy or of benefit; it would be right for us to consider him equal to the Beginning of all things, if not indeed by nature, certainly in usefulness; for when everything was falling [into disorder] and tending

---

[1] Professor Ronald Mellor of UCLA's History Department read the complete paper and offered many helpful suggestions. This paper was written in 1991.

toward dissolution, he restored it once more and gave to the whole world a new aspect; it might have wished for death, had not Caesar been born, the common good fortune of all. One may therefore rightly view as the Beginning of life and of vitality what has given to the misery of being born an end and a limit. ... it is my wish that all the cities unanimously adopt the birthday of divine Caesar as the new beginning of the year ....[2]

And then the Provincial Assembly of the Province of Asia decreed:

Whereas the Province which has regulated our whole existence, and which has shown such care and liberality, has brought our life to the climax of perfection in giving to us [the emperor] Augustus, whom it [Providence] filled with virtue for the welfare of men, and who, being sent to us and our descendants as a Savior, has put an end to war and has set all things in order ... and whereas, finally, the birthday of the god [Augustus] has been for the whole world the beginning of good news concerning him [therefore, let a

---

[2]As found in Frederick C. Grant, *Ancient Roman Religion* (New York: Liberal Arts Press, 1957) 173-174. Brackets belong to Grant.

new era begin from his birth, and let his birthday mark the beginning of the new year].³

The Provincial Assembly of Asia gave Augustus divine honors because they perceived him to be the restorer of order and peace.

One can also find praises among Roman poets. In *Carmen Saeculare*, Horace alludes to the restoration of Augustus:

> And what the glorious son of Anchises and Venus [i.e. Augustus] asks of you, with a sacrifice of white steers, that grant to him, victorious over the warring, but generous to the defeated! .... Even now Faith and Peace and Honor and ancient Shame and neglected Virtue are venturing to return, and blessed Abundance with her full horn manifests herself. May Phoebus the Prophet ... look with favor upon the altars on the Palatine Mount, continue Rome's wealth and Latium's prosperity, to new periods and ages ever better.⁴

Horace thus writes with hope concerning Rome's future.

Virgil also writes on a positive note concerning the future of Rome because Augustus was now in power. Virgil writes in *Eclogues*, IV. 788:

---

³As found in Grant, 174. Brackets belong to Grant.
⁴As found in Grant, 184. Brackets belong to Grant.

> Turn now and look with both your eyes: behold this people, your own Romans! Here is Caesar, and all of Iulus's posterity, destined to appear under the mighty vault of heaven. And here is he, the one you have so often heard promised you, Augustus Caesar, the son of a god, who shall once more reestablish the Age of Gold in Latium, over the fields where once Saturn reigned ....[5]

Thus, one can see that poets portrayed Augustus as a restorer of order and re-establisher of the glorious past.

In the eyes of those living in the Roman Empire, Augustus ended civil strife and brought peace. Augustan era, in contrast with the late Republic, indeed appeared to be a golden age. William Halliday describes the situation in the late Republic: "The misery of the last hundred years of the Republic is indisputable. It is a century of revolutions, civil wars and proscriptions, a period of complete anarchy when neither life nor property were secure."[6] Roman religion was also in a sad state. Gaston Boissier describes: "... la décadence de la religion romaine était visible, elle devait frapper et inquiéter les esprits

---

[5] As found in Grant, 211.
[6] *Lectures on the History of Roman Religion from Numa to Augustus* (Liverpool: University Press of Liverpool, 1922) 132.

prévoyants."⁷ Anything seemed better compared to the disorder of the late Republic.

Not only did Augustus brought peace, he enacted religious legislations, rebuilt temples, and reintroduced some of the neglected practices of previous Rome. This has caused some historians to comment that Augustus attempted to restore traditional Roman religions. Franz Cumont writes: "It is well known that Augustus, prompted by political rather than by religious reasons, attempted to revive the dying religion."⁸ Also, Halliday writes: "Though Augustus was not a religious man himself, he may well have been sincere in his belief that a healthier tone might be restored by getting back to the old [Roman] religion."⁹ Furthermore, Boissier writes: "Auguste travailla pendant tout son regne a restaurer la religion romaine et à lui rendre l'autorité qu'elle avait perdue."¹⁰ Although they may disagree on Augustus' intention, all of the historians mentioned above hold that Augustus was trying to revive, or restore, the traditional Roman religion. Underlying this assumption is the idea that traditional Roman religions could be revived or restored.

But the traditional Roman religion was not something that could be revived or restored because it was syncretistic polytheism. Augustan age was not a period of religious revival in the way that the Great

---

⁷*La Religion Romaine d'Auguste aux Antonins* (Paris: Librairie Hachette, 1874) 47.
⁸*The Oriental Religions in Roman Paganism* (New York: Dover Publications, 1956) 30.
⁹163.
¹⁰74.

Awakening is perceived to be a period of religious revival in America. Alan Wardman attributes misunderstanding of Augustan religious "revival" to the fact that historians of ancient Roman history have been too eager to accept Augustan writers' words concerning the Republican era. Wardman writes: "Historians have also been too ready to accept the verdict of the Augustan writers on the late Republic as an age of religious decline."[11]

J. H. W. G. Liebeschuetz is another scholar who is not ready to accept the idea of religious decline of the late Republic too easily. He argues for religiosity of a traditional kind in the late Republic. Liebeschuetz writes: "A visitor to the Rome of the late republic would still observe a vast amount of traditional ritual. Apart from numerous festivals, every public act began with a religious ceremony, just as the agenda of every meeting of the senate was headed by religious business."[12]

Therefore, Wardman offers an alternative understanding of Roman religiosity. He explains that there could be a decline and incline at the same time in polytheism. Wardman writes:

> Augustan creativity in religion is better interpreted in the light of assumptions which define civic polytheism as subject to unstable increase and decrease at one and the same time. A

---

[11] *Religions and Statecraft among the Romans* (London: Granada, 1982) 64.
[12] *Continuity and Change in Roman Religion* (Oxford: Oxford University Press, 1979) 1.

useful way to interpret polytheism is to see it as a bulge-and-squeeze religion, not as a religion which either expands all over or declines in the same way.[13]

But Wardman points out that the term "revival" may be useful when used carefully to mean exposing populace to certain practices and experiences so that they can be shared evenly; for, in a polytheistic society, religious experiences are uneven among the citizens.[14]

Thus, although it is not appropriate to refer to Augustan religious activities as "revival" of traditional religion with a Judeo-Christian frame of mind, it is certain that Augustus did reintroduced to the populace practices from traditional Roman religions that have been neglected by most of the Roman populace for some time. Not only that, Augustus rebuilt temples and introduced innovative modifications of traditional Roman religions. Boissier describes Augustus' religious activities: "Il a tout à la fois le goût de l'ancien et du nouveau; il aime sans doute à revenir au passé; mais pour qu'il reprenne son élan et son ardeur, quand il les a perdus, il est bon que le passé soit rejeuni pas quelques innovations."[15]

Whether reintroduction or innovation of the traditional Roman religions, Augustus carried in all his deeds a political purpose for himself. Halliday writes: "We must look more probably for political

---

[13]64.
[14]Wardman, 65.
[15]78.

motives and in religious policy, as elsewhere, we may admire the astonishing dexterity, the long views and the almost uncannily skilful adoption of means to his end which characterised Augustus' work."[16]

But this was in keeping with the Roman way of life. For Romans, religious and political life has always been intricately intertwined. Liebescheutz shows this by pointing out that political manipulation of religion during the late Republic should not be seen as a moral decline; rather, there was a change in the nature of manipulation, and not in the fundamental relationship between religious and political life. Liebescheutz writes:

> It has often been suggested that the political exploitation of religion in the late republic is a symptom of religious decay. This is probably a mistake. There were changes in the way religion was exploited in Roman politics, but the fact of its exploitation goes back as far as our information about the politics of Rome.[17]

Thus, one can see that religious policies were intricately related with political life.

Liebeschuetz gives one typical example of this. He feels that the institution of divination was a political vehicle to maintain peace and give power to local magistrates. Liebeschuetz writes:

---

[16] 160.
[17] 20.

> To sum up: a principal purpose of the institution was to preserve morale and to prevent panic among the populace at large in times of stress. More specifically, divination contributed to the reverence and confidence with which the political institutions were regarded. It gave greater authority to the magistrates elected by the people and to the decisions made by them.[18]

Divination, therefore, propped up political authority.

Augustus, too, manipulated religion for his political purposes, but he did it ingeniously. First of all, Augustus portrayed himself as concerned with traditional religion by getting actively involved in the religious scene.

Augustus became *pontifex maximus*, but he was careful to show that he did not eliminate anybody to hold this office. He waited patently until the position was vacated by the former *pontifex maximus*. Augustus writes in the *Res Gestae*:

> I declined to become *pontifex maximus* in place of a colleague while he was still alive, when the people offered me that priesthood, which my father had held. A few years later, in the consulship of Publius Suplicius and Gaius Valgius, I accepted this priesthood, when death removed the man who had taken possession of it at a

---

[18] 16.

> time of civil disturbance; and from all Italy a multitude flocked to my election such as had never previously been recorded at Rome.[19]

The office of *pontifex maximus* meant a lot for Augustus, so that Augustus waited patiently for it. Boissier explains: "Une seule fonction lui manquait pour être le chef de la religion romaine, celle de grand pontife: Il l'attendit longtemps, et, ce qui lui fait honneur, il eut la patience de l'attendre."[20]

The office of *pontifex maximus* provided Augustus with the highest religious authority. Thus, the highest religious and civil authority was combined in Augustus. Boissier describes: "Ainsi furent réunies dans la même main le puissance religieuse et l'autorité civile."[21]

Augustus' hold on this office is significant because since the late Republic, the *pontifices* have provided a good example of the religious manipulation of the political process. Because the *pontifices* held the control of the Roman calendar, they were able to manipulate the dates allowed for assembly for decision making purposes. Liebeschuetz writes:

> Much of the evidence for the importance of religion in the public life of

---

[19]As found in Ronald Mellor (ed.), *From Augustus to Nero: The First Dynasty of Imperial Rome* (East Lansing: Michigan State University Press, 1990) 36.
[20]93.
[21]94.

the late republic shows it being manipulated for partisan political purposes. In fact religious manipulation can be said to have a recognized place in the Roman constitution. So the Roman calendar, supervised by the *pontifices* could and did manipulate the insertion of intercalary months in such a way as to provide more or less time for legislation, or to extend or reduce the tenure of a particular office holder, or the length of a particular public contract. The time available for legislation or for political trials could also be affected by the proclamation of a period of public thanksgiving, or the discovery that a festival had been celebrated incorrectly and must be performed again.[22]

Augustus had possession of this powerful office.
    As the chief religious authority in Rome, Augustus performed works of restoration. For example, Augustus repaired temples. In the *Res Gestae*, Augustus boasts: "In my sixth consulship I repaired eighty-two temples of the gods in the city, in accordance with a resolution of the senate, neglecting none which at that time required repair."[23] When one reads this, one may attribute to Augustus' repairs greater praise than that which is deserved.

---

[22] 2.
[23] As found in Mellor, 38.

When one reads about Augustus' repairs of eighty-two temples, one must be careful to catch possible exaggerations. After all, the year in which the repairs were done is significant. The alleged repairs in Augustus' sixth consulship, 28 B.C., marked the end of a civil war, victory over Cleopatra, and the year that the great "restoration" of Augustus was to begin. Because of the propagandist nature surrounding the repairs, one must be sceptical about exaggerated descriptions concerning disrepair of temples during the Republic.[24]

Also, one must consider the facts surrounding these repairs. These temples were extremely vulnerable to fire from lightning or flooding from the Tiber; thus, there was much need for repair during Augustus' time. Also, the huge number points to the repairs as being minor in nature. Furthermore, these repairs were means of political survival. Popular sentiment in the Roman Empire was that temple in disrepair offends gods. Surely, Augustus did not want to be seen as carelessly offending gods.[25]

Just as Augustus' restoration of the temple had a political motive, Augustus used his office to give the Roman people a personal devotional framework to himself. This can be seen in the issues surrounding the dwelling place of Augustus as a *pontifex maximus*. First of all, Augustus circumvented religious tradition in which *pontifex maximus* was supposed to live in the *Regia* by giving it to Vestal Virgins. This allowed him to increase the importance of Vestal Virgins, as he wished, and also not to live

---

[24]Wardman, 70-71.
[25]Wardman, 71.

in the *Regia*. Augustus was able to live in his new palace on Palatine hill after he declared some of it public land. His own living quarters, therefore, came to have a religious significance for the whole empire.[26]

Liebeschuetz perceives Augustus' efforts to live in his own palace as a preparation for having Romans join in his family worship. Liebeschuetz describes:

> Augustus had been very careful to take preliminary measures so that this extension of his family worship would be formally proper. When Augustus became *pontifex maximus* in 12 B.C. he did not move into the official residence of the head of Roman religion, but instead made part of his house on the Palatine hill public land.[27]

And, indeed, worship of the *genius* of Augustus' household was institutionalized by the senate after Augustus' victory over Antony and Cleopatra. Libation was to be poured to Augustus' *genius* at all public and private banquets.[28]

Augustus did much to encourage people in the Roman empire to participate in his family worship. He even reorganized Rome into different regions to facilitate it. Halliday describes:

---

[26]Halliday, 167.
[27]70.
[28]Liebeschuetz, 68-69.

Augustus now organized Rome into fourteen regions, each of which was subdivided into *vici*. He revived the *collegia compitum* and at the junctions of the boundaries of these subdivisions were erected shrines containing three images. Two represented the Lares; the third associated with them was the Genius of Augustus. The third partner in this triad naturally predominated in popular estimation and the three became known as Lares Augusti.[29]

Augustus' office as *pontifex maximus* provided him with a means to build on the extent of Roman devotion and loyalty to Augustus.

Augustus' efforts to have others identify in his personal and family worship in order to foster loyalty and facilitate his political purposes can be found also in his creative renovating efforts with various deities. He gave public honor to gods who were particularly linked with his own life and career.

Augustus gave special honor to the goddess Venus because of her personal association with the Julian family and also because of the illustrious birth that her deity implied for him. Boissier writes:

> Vénus était regardée comme la mère des Romains, et c'est à ce titre que Lucrèce l'invoque au commencement de son poëme; mais elle était surtout la

---

[29]176.

mère de la famille des Jules, qui se prétendaient issus d'Énée. Octave aussi était très-fier de cette illustre naissance et pendant les premiers temps de son pouvoir, l'image de *Venus Genetrix* paraît souvent sur ses monnaies.[30]

Thus, Augustus wanted gods personally associated with him to be honored.

Augustus also creatively renovated the cult of Mars the Avenger, in association with his campaigns against murderers of Julius Caesar. In 42 B.C., before the battle of Philippi, Augustus vowed a temple to Mars if the battle result in avenging of Julius Caesar's death. In 20 B.C., he built shrine on the Capitol to house the standards of Crassus which diplomacy had recovered from Parthians. And then in 2 B.C., Augustus consecrated a temple of Mars in the new forum. Building a temple for Mars was an innovative concept. Many Italian peoples worshipped Mars, but as a wild spirit outside of the city needed for war campaigns. Liebeschuetz describes the significance of Augustus' act:

> Augustus also promoted Mars. Mars was worshipped by many Italian peoples and he had always figured in the religious history of Rome, but in a special way. He had no temple within the *pomerium*. He was treated as a wild spirit, whose help was needed but

---
[30] 79.

> who had to be kept at a distance. His help was needed on campaigns -- but outside the city. Augustus brought him into the city and made his temple a memorial to the qualities that had made Rome great. He built the temple on land owned by himself. This was appropriate because his motives for honouring the god were in the first place personal. He was honouring the god who had helped him to avenge his father's murder.[31]

Augustus, therefore, successfully translated personal relationship with Mars, who avenged his father's death, into public devotion.

Also, based on personal experiences, Augustus gave special recognition to Apollo. Augustus narrowly escaped being killed by lightning in 36 B.C., and he gave gratitude to Apollo. Five years later, Augustus's victory over Antony and Cleopatra was won near a well-known sanctuary of Apollo at Actium. Augustus claimed that Apollo helped him to win this important battle. Thus, Augustus portrayed Apollo as his protector. Liebeschuetz notes: "It looks as if Augustus genuinely believed that Apollo was his personal protector."[32]

Because Augustus viewed Apollo as his personal protector, he preferred him over all other gods. Boissier writes: "Le culte d'Apollon Palatin était plus personnel à l'empereur que les deux autres.

---

[31] 86.
[32] 83.

Auguste paraît avoir eu de toute temps pour Apollon une dévotion particulière...."[33]

Thus, Augustus took particular care in fostering public devotion to the god who was protecting him personally. He built a temple of Apollo on Palatine. Boissier describes the beauty of the temple on the consecrated land: "C'est sur ce terrain que fut construit le temple célèbre d'Apollon Palatin: c'était un édifice magnifique, de marbre de Carare, rempli des chefs-d'œuvre de l'art grec et surmonté d'une statue du soleil sur un quadrige d'or."[34] Augustus transferred the Sibylline books from the temple of Jupiter Optimus Maximus to this new temple. Furthermore, he involved the Secular Games in a ceremony in the temple of Apollo. Thus, Apollo enjoyed public devotion as the supporter of the Roman state, although he had previously only minor role as a god of healing.[35]

Halliday succinctly summarizes Augustus' successful efforts to direct public devotion to gods associated with him personally: "Augustus thus associated himself with the state religion, emphasised the importance of deities especially connected with his family or his career and made his domestic hearth equivalent to the hearth of the state."[36]

Not only did Augustus elicit public devotion for gods associated personally with his life or experience, he encouraged the veneration of deified Julius Caesar, his father. Worship of Julius Caesar

---

[33]80.
[34]81.
[35]Liebeschuetz, 83.
[36]172.

started among the Romans soon after the death of Julius Caesar. Augustus played his political cards shrewdly by timely institutionalizing the worship. Liebeschuetz describes:

> A cult of Julius Caesar arose, it seems spontaneously, soon after his murder, and was thought to have received supernatural confirmation when a comet was seen during seven nights while the Ludi Victoriae Caesaris were being celebrated. This provided an opportunity for Octavian ... to proclaim that the comet was Caesar's soul, and to give wide publicity to the claim by attaching stars to statues of Caesar. Thus, Octavian could begin his political career with the unique advantage of having a god for a father. It is not surprising that among the first acts of the second Triumvirate was the establishment of formal state cult for the dead Caesar.[37]

One can see that Augustus was effective in using religious devotion to his dead father for political advantage.

  Politically, Augustus was a very shrewd man; he understood the intricate relationship between Roman religion and politics. Therefore, Augustus directed Roman religiosity toward gods related with his life or experience. In the process, he not only revived

---

[37] 65--66.

some of the neglected aspects of traditional Roman religion, but also creatively renovated certain aspects of religion and worship for his political end.

Bibliography

Primary Sources

Grant, Frederick C. *Ancient Roman Religion.* New York: Liberal Arts Press, 1957.

Mellor, Ronald (ed.). *From Augustus to Nero: The First Dynasty of Imperial Rome.* East Lansing, MI: Michigan State University Press, 1990.

Secondary Sources

Basanoff, V. *Les Dieux des Romains.* Paris: Presses Universitaires de France, 1942.

Bayet, Jean. *Histoire Politique et Psychologique de la Religion Romaine.* Paris: Payot, 1969.

Boissier, Gaston. *La Religion Romaine d'Auguste aux Antonins.* Paris: Librairie Hachette, 1874.

Halliday, William. *Lectures on the History of Roman Religion from Numa to Augustus.* Liverpool: University Press of Liverpool, 1922.

Liebeschuetz, J. H. W. G. *Continuity and Change in Roman Religion.* Oxford: Oxford University Press, 1979.

Wardman, Alan. *Religion and Statecraft among the Romans.* London: Granada, 1982.

"A Review of Caroline Walker Bynum's
*Holy Feast and Holy Fast:
The Religious Significance
of Food to Medieval Women*"[1]

Caroline Walker Bynum's book, *Holy Feast and Holy Fast: The Religious Significance of Food to Medieval Women* (Berkeley: University of California Press, 1987), takes a bold step arguing for the religious significance of food in the Middle Ages in general and for the medieval women in particular. She utilizes research in the social and religious areas of medieval life to prove her point. She is largely successful. However, due to the nature of the task, her efforts are not flawless.

Bynum's intention for her book is evident in her introduction. Bynum stresses the importance of food in the religious atmosphere of the Middle Ages, particularly for women. She writes: "Not only was food a more significant motif in late medieval spirituality than most historians have recognized, food was also a more important motif in women's piety than in men's" (4). Therefore, she points out that "... women's behavior and women's writing must be understood in the context of social, economic, and ecclesiastical structures, theological and devotional traditions, very different from our own" (9). Thus, she calls for sensitivity to the medieval understanding

---

[1] This was written in 1991. Professor Robert Benson of UCLA's History Department offered helpful comments.

of the significance of food and its significance for medieval women.

This is a bold step. She is going against some of the traditional historical research concerning food and women. Formerly, historians did not attribute such a great religious significance of food for women, which Bynum claims. Bynum points out that many historians perceived religious practices, such as fasting, as an inherent flaw in the women of the Middle Ages, or in the environment around them. Bynum writes:

> The interpretation historians of religion have given to this phenomenon has been monolithic -- so much so that it has come to seem common sense. Late medieval women hated their bodies and their sexuality, we are told, and punished them through fasting and other forms of self-mutilation. They internalized a misogyny to which the philosophical, scientific, theological, and folk traditions and the structures of church and society all contributed. Some historians have responded to women's ascetic practices with embarrassment or even anger; others have responded with compassion. Conservative historians of theology have sometimes blamed the women. Historians of medicine of psychiatry have sometimes blamed society. Marxist and feminist historians have often

> blamed the church. But, whatever its cause, women's asceticism has seemed to modern scholars self-evidently dualistic and pathological -- an effort to flee or destroy the flesh so that the spirit might return to God (208-9).

In light of former historiography on the subject, Bynum's innovative efforts in the book are a great contribution.

Bynum shows that food is religiously significant for women in three ways: not eating, feeding, and eating. And it was more significant for women than for men. She writes: "Throughout the Middle Ages, however, preachers associated religious food practices -- especially charitable food distribution, fasting, and eucharistic fervor -- with women" (80). She discusses each of these in the context of the social and religious atmosphere of the times.

Fasting comprised an important part of the medieval religious culture. But Bynum argues that it was particularly significant for women. Women of the Middle Ages were practicing extreme fasting and perceived themselves as participating in the cross of Jesus Christ. Bynum explains: "[Fasting] was identification with Christ's suffering; it was effective, even erotic, union with Christ's adorable self" (120).

Furthermore, they saw their fasting as a service of others in that they partook of the pains of purgatory. Purgatory, for medieval women, was not a place between heaven and hell; rather, purgatory "... simply *was* suffering -- redemptive suffering -- which was simultaneously Christ's and the sinner's. Thus suffering on earth could replace suffering later, and by suffering one could redeem others as well as oneself" (120 Italics not mine). Thus, women placed great emphasis on fasting.

Bynum argues that men in the Middle Ages did not attribute the same degree of importance to fasting. In fact, some even hindered extreme fasting of women. For example, Francis of Assisi forbade Clare of Assisi from fasting totally for three days; rather, he required her to take an ounce and a half of bread each day. Bynum feels that this clearly shows the distinction in the roles fasting played for men and women of the time. Bynum writes:

> Raised in the same small Italian city, tributary to the same spiritual currents, influenced by each other, Clare and Francis expressed the same craving for self-abnegation and world denial. But they expressed it in different behaviors and metaphors. Only to Clare was food crucial. Francis renounced wealth; Clare renounced food (102).

For Bynum, this explains why most stories relating Francis with food deal with his eating and not with his fasting (96).

Medieval women attributed religious significance to feeding along side of fasting; in fact, they went hand in hand. There was a spiritual significance in the feeding of pious women. Although the pious women abstained from earthly food, by participating in the suffering of Jesus Christ, and, thereby, in his body-broken, they became food. Bynum writes: "Medieval women fed others. They abstained in order to feed others. They fed others with their own bodies.... In a fierce imitation of the cross ... women became the macerated body of the Savior ..." (114). Thus, Bynum comments that, "Indeed, Colette *became* food" (139 Italics not mine). The pious women offered their bodies as spiritual food through suffering and service of others. Bynum explains: "The communication of God to humanity and the giving of one self to another through suffering or service is understood as 'feeding' -- an imparting of flesh that nurtures as it is consumed" (135).

    Feeding did not merely belong to the spiritual realm; these women did, in fact, feed the hungry. Some religious women not only gave what they had, they went beyond, and sacrificed their time, effort, and pride to bring food to the poor. One such person was Mary of Oignies, who denigrated herself to feed others. Bynum describes: "Mary of Oignies, who never achieved the complete poverty she wanted, gave her own goods to the poor, begged in order to feed them, and worked for their food ..." (121).

    Sometimes, feeding was done miraculously. Bynum accounts a food multiplication miracle, like Jesus' miracle of the loaves and fishes, done by Umiltà of Faenza. Another miraculous feeding found expression in women becoming a source of food that has miraculous healing powers. Bynum writes: "Most remarkable of all, the women's bodies themselves became a source of food. They exuded oil, milk, or sweet saliva that had the power to cure others" (122). Another miraculous nature of feeding can be found in the belief that dead women saints fed others. Bynum writes: "Holy women continued to feed others miraculously from beyond the grave" (123). It is evident that feeding had a great religious significance for women, both socially and religiously.

Closely associated with the religious significance of fasting and feeding was the female religiosity present in eating, especially at the Eucharist. In fact, women saints fasted to make their eucharistic experience more poignant. Then, these saints fed others. Bynum describes the relationship: "For those in whose lives serving was more important, fasting and Eucharist were the self-denial and self-replenishment that made the feeding of others possible" (130).

But the Eucharist, itself, held a great religious significance for women. Bynum comments: "In particular, the Eucharist was associated with female saints" (81). Miracles associated with the Eucharist were more commonplace for women than for men. For some, eucharistic food replaced normal food as nurture. In a sense, all the fasting before the Eucharist, found its physical satisfaction in it. Furthermore, there were visions associated with the Eucharist. Some women received visions of Christ in the host at the elevation. Adelheid Langemann thought that she was married to Jesus with the host as the sign of the marriage rather than with a ring. Also, eucharistic visions provided religious women with social power -- the wherewithal to ascertain the purity and sanctity of the priests administering the Eucharist. The Eucharist, and eating associated with it, clearly had significance for religiosity of medieval women.

Caroline Walker Bynum, therefore, undertook the great task of showing the religious significance of food and, particularly, its manifestation in women through their not eating, feeding, and eating. Much praise is due for her research, which in its enormity parallels the task of her book. For example, she must be praised for incorporating much original writings of women -- such as of Hadewijch, Beatrice of Nazareth, Catherine of Siena, and Catherine of Genoa -- to show the religious significance of food to medieval women. Furthermore, her comparative study, such as between Francis and Clare of Assisi, proves most valuable in ascertaining differing male and female emphases on food.

But one cannot give unreserved praise for Bynum's book; there are some weaknesses. First of all, Bynum is repetitive and unclear in her approach. For example, Bynum repeats her thesis frequently and along with this, criticism of former historiography on the subject. Thus, one finds her criticizing historical explanations of fasting women as having emotional or mental problems. But Bynum, in turn, devotes several chapters on the theme of control that women experienced, actually or psychologically, in regards to food. Bynum believes that women's only social means of control was through preparing, eating, and feeding food. Thus, food played a significant role in the psyche of medieval women. Elaborate religiosity developed around food, and with this religiosity, women's power developed through control of food. This shows that Bynum falls into her own criticism of others for confining women in the sociological framework of the time and stripping women of any real characteristic religious significance.

Secondly, Bynum has some misinformation in her book. One example found in Bynum's assessment that "In Old Testament Judaism, fasting is almost the only religious act for which women (e.g., Judith, Esther, Sarah, the mothers of Samuel and Samson) are prominent models of piety" (192). This is just not true.

It would be appropriate to take one case and examine carefully to see whether Bynum's argument is correct. Here is the account of Hannah, the mother of Samuel, and the account of her fasting:

> [Elkanah] had two wives; one was called Hannah and the other Peninnah. Peninnah had children, but Hannah had none. .... And because the LORD had closed her womb, her rival kept provoking her in order to irritate her. This went on year after year. Whenever Hannah went up to the house of the LORD, her rival provoked her till she wept and would not eat. Elkanah her husband would say to her. "Hannah, why are you weeping? Why don't you eat? Why are you downhearted? Don't I mean more to you than than sons?" Once when they had finished eating and drinking in Shiloh, Hannah sood up. Now Eli the priest

was sitting on a chair by the doorpost of the LORD's temple. In bitterness of soul Hannah wept much and prayed to the LORD. .... As she kept on praying to the LORD, Eli observed her mouth. Hannah was praying in her heart, and her lips were moving but her voice was not heard. Eli thought she was drunk and said to her, "How long will you keep on getting drunk? Get rid of your wine." "Not so, my lord," Hannah replied, "I am a woman who is deeply troubled. I have not been drinking wine or beer; I was pouring out my soul to the LORD. Do not take your servant for a wicked woman; I have been praying here out of my great anguish and grief. Eli answered, "Go in peace, and may the God of Israel grant you what you have asked of him" (I Samuel 1:2, 6-10, 12-17 NIV).

When one examines this text carefully, one can see that Hannah's fasting is not exhibited as an exemplary religious act; rather, it is a puerile response to Peninnah's teasing her concerning her barrenness. Her husband even reprimands her and encourages her to eat. And in verse 9, one can see that both Hannah and her husband ate. After they ate together, Hannah got up and went to the temple to pray. Hannah was praying intently to the extent that Eli the priest thought she was drunk. Upon inquiry, Eli assessed

Hannah's wishes and requests before God; therefore, Eli grants Hannah's wishes. Perhaps her intensity of prayer is set up as a religious example, but certainly not her fasting. Hannah's fasting is a childish response that Hannah's husband reprimands.

Furthermore, Bynum's book would have been much more effective, had she provided a firmer foundation for the idea of the religiosity of food for women. Are there some significant traces of develop-ment in early Christianity, the patristic period, or even the early Middle Ages? She gives basic examples of the fast of Jesus and the communion as precedents for the religious significance of food for women. This is inadequate; there is too much of a gap between this and her thesis.

Yet, one cannot be too critical of Bynum's work; for it was a bold attempt in the uncharted waters. But one must also ask oneself: Does that justify her misinformation, repetition, and not providing adequate religio-historical and theological foundations for the religious significance of food for women? One is left to answer "no."

"Syriac Spirituality:
Clothing and Nakedness as Symbolic Reality"[1]

The symbolism of clothing and nakedness presents itself powerfully in Syriac Christianity, perhaps the part of the nascent Christian movement most influenced by Jewish traditions. In the salvation history and spiritual expression of Syriac Christians, clothing imagery functions as a reality integral to personal identity and experience and grants one entrance to sacred time and space. The Adam typology, which plays an important role in Syriac Christian thinking, is also understood in terms of clothing imagery. The firm-rootedness of clothing imagery in the Syriac Christian psyche becomes even more evident upon a closer examination of the liturgical text, *Anaphora of Addai and Mari*, and of an excerpt from the hagiography called, "Mary, Niece of Abraham of Qidun." The examination of these texts would be better served if one looks at the historical and experiential context of Syriac Christianity.

It is in Antioch that followers of Jesus of Nazareth are first called "Christians" according to Acts 11:26. But Gelston does not believe that East

---

[1] This paper was written at the Hebrew University of Jerusalem, where I was a Visiting Research Fellow for the 1993-94 academic year. I would like to thank The Goldsmith Foundation and the State of Israel for their financial support. I would also like to acknowledge with thanks Professor Michael Stone and Professor David Satran of the Comparative Religions Department at the Hebrew University of Jerusalem who read the complete draft of the paper and offered many helpful comments.

Syrian Christianity had its origin in Antioch; rather, its origins are "lost in obscurity." What is certain is that the division between East Syrians and West Syrians came as the result of the Christological controversies of the fifth century, particularly instigated by the Council of Ephesus in 431 AD. The second half of the century saw Monophysites in power in Edessa and East Syrians, who followed the teachings of Theodore of Mopsuestia, withdrawn into Persia. Thus, Nisibis became the main East Syrian theological center. Political factors, then, contributed to a prolonged separation of the East Syrian Church from the rest of Christendom.[2] Yet, in terms of spiritual experience and expression, these two differed little, if at all. Their foundational heritage held firm within the core of their spirituality.

What was their heritage? Scholars are mostly agreed on the integral influence of Jewish traditions on Syrian Christianity. In his discussion of the Jewish influence on Syriac Christianity, Brock points to four main areas of Syriac literature exhibiting Jewish traits. First, Jewish traditions were incorporated into the actual Syriac translations of the Hebrew Scriptures, most noticeably in the Pentateuch and Chronicles. Secondly, early Syriac writings show indebtedness to targumic traditions, although such heritage is absent from the extant Peshitta text of the Bible. Third, the value that Syriac Christianity attached to Jewish traditions exhibits itself in the preservation in

---

[2]A. Gelston, *The Eucharistic Prayer of Addai and Mari* (Oxford: Clarendon Press, 1992) 21-22.

the Syriac language[3] of the apocrypha and pseudepigrapha of Jewish origin, some of which only survive in Syriac. Fourthly, certain types of Syriac literature, like commentaries, poetry, chronicles, and "hagiography" of the Hebrew Scriptures, further show Jewish influence.[4] One can see the pervasiveness of the Jewish influence on Syriac Christianity.

Another scholar also attaches a great significance to the influence of Jewish traditions on Syriac Christianity; Gelston comments that the influence from Judaism is one of the three important factors to keep in mind when reading the Anaphora of Addai and Mari.[5] Brock and Harvey also greatly emphasizes the Jewish heritage of Syriac Christianity: "Christianity first emerged in the Syriac Orient out of the Jewish communities, largely independent of the Graeco-Latin churches to the west, and with a

---

[3] The Syriac language, which developed specifically as a language of Christian peoples and maintained as such by Christians in the eastern Mediterranean realm, originated in the region of Edessa (modern Urfa, in southeast Turkey) as a dialect of Aramaic, the language of the first-century Palestine. Syriac spread especially in the first two centuries of the Common Era (Sebastian P. Brock and Susan A. Harvey, *Holy Women of the Syrian Orient* {Berkeley and Los Angeles: University of California Press, 1987} 4).

[4] "Jewish Traditions in Syriac Sources," *Journal of Jewish Studies* (XXX, 1979, pp. 212-232) 212.

[5] 23. Another factor is the emphasis on apostolic authority. This is evidenced in that the *Anaphora of Addai and Mari* is named after Addai, the traditional apostle of Edessa, and his disciple, Mari. Furthermore, the earliest texts of the anaphora is simply named, "The Sanctification of the Apostles." The third factor is the existence of a common core with the Maronite anaphora *Sharar*. The significance of this factor will be discussed in length later in the text of this paper.

powerful spirituality born of semitic tradition rather than that of classical Greece and Rome."[6] For Brock and Harvey, this Jewish influence was exclusive of Hellenistic influence: "From its semitic roots Syriac Christianity inherited biblical tradition directly from Judaism. That is to say, where the Greek and Latin churches dealt with Judaism in its Diaspora form, with the influences of Hellenic thought and culture and particularly the impact of philosophy...."[7]

Currently there are discussions of whether one can distinguish between the Hellenistic Diaspora and pure Judaism unaffected by Hellenism. These scholars point to the reality of Hellenism as a cultural phenomenon, unrestricted by geographical boundary within the eclectic world. Some have even questioned pure Jewishness of the Qumran community and point to some possible Hellenistic influences. For example, one of the obvious characteristics of the Greek ways of thinking is in categories. Therefore, one would ask, "What are the qualities that make something what that is?" Bertold Gärtner, therefore, points to the self-attribution of temple qualities within Qumran literature and argues that the Qumran community perceived itself as a "new temple," on which the *Shakinah* of God dwelled.[8] This shows us that even a community that one would normally perceive as having actively worked to remain purely

---

[6] Brock and Harvey 6.
[7] 7.
[8] See chapter three of Bertil Gärtner's book, *The Temple and the Community in Qumran and the New Testament*, which is titled "The 'New Temple' in Qumran" (Cambridge: At the University Press, 1965).

Jewish had influences from Hellenistic ways of thinking; namely, in categories. This leads one to question Brock and Harvey's statement concerning the absence of Hellenistic influence on early Syriac Christianity.[9] But their point is well taken: Jewish traditions had a great influence on Syriac Christianity. And this will become even more evident throughout the paper.

Thus, it is not surprising that the pre-fall purity is a theme of great interest within Syriac Christianity; the idea of going back to pre-fall Adam state. That concerned the core of Syriac spirituality, rather than the focus on salvation as a distinct reality away

---

[9]Brock does recognize "Greek" influence on Syriac Christianity. In his article, "Jewish Traditions in Syriac Sources," Brock states that Greek culture became the predominantly influential tradition from the fifth century onwards because of its prestige. But Brock argues that Jewish tradition exerted continued influence on Syriac Christianity until the Islamic period and that this tradition was the most influential before the fifth century (212). In another article, however, Brock recognizes an earlier Greek influence. The earliest non-biblical translations from Greek were being made even during Ephrem's lifetime in the fourth century. These translations include works by Eusebius and writings of Titus of Bostra against the Manichaeans. Soon, translations of Greek patristic writers followed. Brock comments on the immediate influence of the Greek tradition, following its entrance to Syriac Christianity via translations: "It was not long before Greek modes of thought and expression made themselves at home in native Syriac literature" ("Greek into Syriac and Syriac into Greek," *Journal of the Syriac Academy* {III, 1977, pp. 422-406} 422. Note on the reverse paging: the journal is an Arabic journal and is, therefore, paged from right to left, contrary to the paging in western scholarship; thus, when an article written in a western language is published in the Arabic journal, it takes reverse paging.).

from Jewish traditions, as Marcion was prone to emphasize. One may study this Syriac spirituality in two categories; namely, asceticism and poetry. Asceticism in Syriac Christianity is not the kind with which those of us familiar with western Christianity would readily identify. Ascetics in Syriac Christianity did not necessarily go out into the dessert as St. Anthony did. They sometimes stood on a high pillar for all to see, as did Simon the Stylite (389-459), who stood on a sixty-feet-high narrow pillar for forty years.[10] Others walked around naked, as a testimony to their being clothed with Christ and having returned to the pre-fall state. Some even went further in their physical symbolism of having returned to the Paradise by surviving only on wild fruits and water, living among the wild beasts, exposing themselves to different weather conditions, praying constantly and living a life totally devoted to God. They acted out what they perceived as the behavior of Adam and Eve in the Garden of Eden before the Fall.[11]

Such emphasis on living a life worthy of return to the pre-fall Adam stage further exhibited itself in the value Syriac Christianity attached to sexual asceticism. Into the third century and possibly into the fourth century, baptism and the Eucharist were reserved for the sexually celibate.[12] Sexual abstinence, thus, was seen as a necessary component of the Christian life. Thus, it is not surprising that Aphrahat the Persian included sexual denial among the necessary practices for the Christian life. These

---

[10]Brock and Harvey 11.
[11]Brock and Harvey 9.
[12]Brock and Harvey 7-8.

crucial practices are: "pure fasting, pure prayer, love, alms, meekness, virginity, holiness, wisdom, hospitality, simplicity, patience, long suffering, mourning, and purity."[13] This shows that Aphrahat considered virginity as one of the qualities for which one must strive. But one sees from the writings of Aphrahat and also his fourth century contemporary Ephrem that they considered marriage as lawful and permissible. Yet, it is clear that their enthusiasm was for a life of consecration to Christ as a virgin (bṯûlâ; fem. bṯûlṯâ) or "single one" (îhîdayâ). This was the highest charism.[14] This is all understood in light of clothing language. Because the believer is now clothed with the robe of glory lost at the Fall, he or she must live a life worthy of the new clothing. Thus, it is not surprising that the saints in Syriac Christianity were seen as those who successfully preserved their robe of glory until their death. Sexual asceticism was, therefore, at the center of this purity.

Syriac asceticism, thus, can be seen as a part of the process in the regaining of the Paradise. Besides the stress on sexual asceticism was the emphasis on the "imitation of Christ." A believer must participate in the suffering of Christ by mortification and ascetic practices that bring suffering. For Ephrem: "If you truly belong to Christ ... you must clothe yourself in his passion."[15] One sees there that

---

[13]Brock and Harvey 9.
[14]Robert Murray, *Symbols of Church and Kingdom: A Study in Early Syriac Tradition* (Cambridge: Cambridge University Press, 1975) 12.
[15] Sebastian Brock, "Early Syriac Asceticism," *Numen* (XX, 1973, pp. 1-19) 18.

Ephrem uses clothing language to describe the believer's relationship to Christ's suffering. One clearly sees the integral role of clothing imagery in Syriac asceticism.

Clothing language was also important in the other form of Syriac spirituality -- poetic expression. Aphrahat and Ephrem of the fourth century, whom historians perceive as the epitome of Syriac poetic expression, color their writing with clothing symbolism in a way that points to a greater significance of the symbol than as a mere poetic tool. This will become clearer in the examples that will be provided below under the discussion of four-scene salvation history in Syriac Christianity.

In his article, "Clothing Metaphor as a Means of Theological Expression in Syriac Tradition," Brock divides salvation history in Syriac Christianity into four scenes. The first scene concerns Adam and Eve before their fall. They are in Paradise, clothed in "robes of glory." This terminology has its origin in Genesis 3:21: "The LORD God made garments of skin for Adam and his wife and clothed them" (NIV). In the Septuagint and Peshitta, one finds literal translation, but the Targum tradition, both Babylonian and Palestinian, provides "garments of glory." Also, according to Midrash Genesis Rabba 20:12, Rabbi Meir supposedly had a manuscript in which "skin" was absent, and in its place was the word "light." The existence of the concept of the garment of glory or light is particularly significant in the context of the parallel exegetical tradition that existed with the generally understood Jewish and Christian interpretation of Genesis 3:21, that states that God clothed

Adam and Eve's nakedness after the fall. This parallel interpretation understands the verbs in the verse as pluperfects, thus referring to God's action before the fall, at the creation. This rendering became popular within the largely lost apocryphal Adam and Eve literature. And an example of this can be found in the so-called *Apocalypse of Moses*, in which Eve braids the serpent: "Why have you done this to me, in that I have been deprived of the glory with which I was clothed?"[16] Another Jewish source shows similarity with the apocryphal Adam and Eve literature. The *Zohar* states: "Before the Fall; they were dressed in garments of light, but after their trespass in garments of skin" (I.36b). These sources provide needed evidence for the existence and influence of the alternative interpretation of Genesis 3:21 within Jewish tradition. Such interpretation, then, expressed itself in Syriac Christianity in a powerful way. Thus, Adam and Eve emerge dressed in robes of glory at creation within the Syriac Christian tradition.[17]

Scene two provides the contrast. At the Fall, Adam and Eve were deprived of their garments of glory. In contrast to the Greek tradition which concentrates on the robe with which God dresses Adam and Eve after the fall, the Syriac tradition concentrates on the robe of glory of which they were deprived and on the fact that they were stripped of

---

[16] (ed. C. Tischendorff) 20, as quoted in S. Brock's article, "Clothing Metaphors as a Means of Theological Expression in Syriac Tradition," *Typus, Symbol, Allegorie bei den östlichen Vätern und ihren Parallelen im Mittelalter*, ed. Margot Schmidt (Regensburg: Verlag Friedrich Pustet, 1982) 14.

[17] Brock, "Clothing Metaphors as a Means of Theological Expression in Syriac Tradition" 12, 14.

the robe.[18] In Syriac poetic expression, scenes one and two appear together. For instance, Ephrem writes: "Because of that glory with which they were wrapped they felt no shame; but when this was taken away from them after the transgression of the commandment, they felt shame because they had been stripped."[19] One notices that the focus is on the robe of glory and the fact that this creation endowment was stripped at the fall. Solomon of Borsa also writes in his *Book of the Bee*: "Adam and Eve were stripped of the fair glory and the glorious light of purity with which they had been clothed."[20] A Problem arises; namely, there is now a need to recover the robe of glory that is lost. This is especially important because Adam and Eve lost the robe of glory for the rest of humanity. Indeed, salvation history continues in the vein of clothing language and especially in regards to the regaining of the robe of glory.

The central figure in this recovery is Jesus of Nazareth. He enters salvation history in scene three, the incarnation. And even incarnation is expressed in clothing imagery; the Divinity himself[21] put on a

---

[18] Brock, "Clothing Metaphors as a Means of Theological Expression in Syriac Tradition" 12.
[19] *Commentary on Genesis* (ed. R. M. Tonneau) II.14, as provided by S. Brock in "Clothing Metaphors as a Means of Theological Expression in Syriac Tradition" 23.
[20] (ed. E. A. W. Budge) 16, as provided by S. Brock in "Clothing Metaphors as a Means of Theological Expression in Syriac Tradition" 23.
[21] The writer of the paper is sensitive to the current dialogue regarding the gender of God. Yet, for the purposes of this paper,

body.[22] This is more than clearly stated in Syriac Christian sources. It is found in the *Acts of Thomas*: "You are the Son and you put on a body...."[23] Ephrem also states: "The Word in his love bent down and put on the body of humanity so that he might give life to humanity."[24] Here, one sees the intention of the incarnation. Furthermore, Aphrahat writes: "Jesus, because he put on a body and humbled himself, delivered the Church and her children from death."[25] Aphrahat, thus, concludes that the incarnate Word fulfilled his intention of incarnation because he put on a body and humbled himself. Putting on a body plays a significant role; "humbling

---

he has opted to accept the masculine attribution of God, which was used by Syriac writers themselves.

[22] Brock, "Clothing Metaphors as a Means of Theological Expression in Syriac Tradition" 12. In the same article, Brock notes that the phrase, "put on the body," achieved official status in the rendering of *sarkathenta* in the earliest Syriac translation of the Nicene-Constantinopolitan Creed, as accepted by the Persian Church at the Council of Seleucia in 410. This terminology became standard over against the phrase, "put on flesh" (15-16). This language of "putting on a/the body" is especially significant in light of other aspects of Syriac thinking, such as the Adam typology, which would have been deficient with the phrase "put on flesh." For, the Word put on the body, that of the First Adam.

[23] (ed. W. Wright) 217, as provided by S. Brock in "Clothing Metaphors as a Means of Theological Expression in Syriac Tradition" 23.

[24] *Homily on the Prologue of John* (ed. J. Lamy) II, col. 511, as provided by S. Brock in "Clothing Metaphors as a Means of Theological Expression in Syriac Tradition" 25.

[25] *Demonstration* XXXI.20, as provided by S. Brock in "Clothing Metaphors as a Means of Theological Expression in Syriac Tradition" 23.

himself" even can be seen as the apostrophe or the result to the putting on of a body.

According to the Syriac Christian tradition, not only did the divinity take on a body to save humanity, but also to redeem Adam. Ephrem describes Jesus as one "who came to find Adam who had got lost, and to return him in the garment of light to Eden."[26] One notes that Adam's redemption is described in clothing imagery. The clothing language also plays an important role in the description of the process of how humanity is restored to the state of being before the fall. This will become even clearer in the discussion of the scene four of salvation history according to the Syriac tradition.

The Divinity took on a body to affect salvation. But how was this redemption to take place? One finds the answer in the fourth scene, the baptism of Jesus of Nazareth. Baptism of Jesus functions as the source for humanity to regain the lost robe of glory. For in his baptism, Jesus sanctified in sacred time all baptismal water with the result that all who are baptized at any point in time regain the robe of glory.[27] Jacob of Serugh writes: "Baptism weaves a garment of living fire for everyone who comes to it."[28] Such concept was not only ideologically held by intellectuals of the Syriac tradition, but also

---

[26] HdVIRG XVI.9, as provided by S. Brock in "Clothing Metaphors as a Means of Theological Expression in Syriac Tradition" 27.
[27] Brock, "Clothing Metaphors as a Means of Theological Expression in Syriac Tradition" 12.
[28] (ed. P. Bedjan) I,196, as provided by S. Brock in "Clothing Metaphors as a Means of Theological Expression in Syriac Tradition" 26-27.

expressed to every individual at baptism in many churches of the Syriac persuasion. At the Syriac Orthodox baptismal service, it is read: "You are anointed a spiritual lamb so that you may put on the robe of glory from the water."[29] Also, in the East Syrian baptismal service, it is prayed to God about those baptized "that they may preserve in purity the robe of glory with which You clothed them in Your mercy."[30] This robe of glory is the one which Jesus placed in the baptismal water in sacred time and space. Jacob of Serugh writes that Jesus "placed in the womb of baptism the robe of glory."[31] Thus, the baptized regains this robe of glory and gains reentrance to the paradise. But this paradise differs from that in which Adam had found himself at the creation; it is perceived as much greater and glorious than its predecessor. This eschatological paradise produces a tension; for, at baptism, the Christian regains his or her robe of glory, but only in potential. The Christian will gain it fully in reality only at the end of time, at the general resurrection. There are, however, those who may anticipate this reality in their life time, such as saints, who maintain their baptismal robe of glory unspotted. Ephrem writes: "Among the saints none is naked, for they have put

---

[29] (Holms edition) 42, as provided by S. Brock in "Clothing Metaphors as a Means of Theological Expression in Syriac Tradition" 27.
[30] (Urmiah edition) 74, as provided by S. Brock in "Clothing Metaphors as a Means of Theological Expression in Syriac Tradition" 27.
[31] (ed. P. Bedjan) I,168, as provided by S. Brock in "Clothing Metaphors as a Means of Theological Expression in Syriac Tradition" 26.

on glory, nor is there any clad in fig leaves, or standing in shame, for they have found, through our Lord, the robe that belongs to Adam and Eve."[32] Although non-saints do not attain their robes of glory in perfection at baptism, Jesus' baptism provides the means for the initiates to start on the road to receiving the perfect robe of glory. Thus, the forth scene of salvation history is the conclusive scene.

Closely tied with the four scene salvation history is the Adam typology. It was the First Adam who, at the creation, wore the robe of glory and it was also he who lost the robe of glory at the fall. This was expounded above in the discussion of scenes one and two of the salvation history. One, however, notices that scenes three and four also integrally involve the First Adam. In Syriac Christianity one understands the incarnation as Divinity taking on a body. In terms of Adam typology, one explains this phenomenon as the Second Adam putting on the body of the First Adam in order to restore the robe of glory to humankind at baptism, which is the fourth scene. There is a close interweaving of identity between the First Adam and the Second Adam, however. God puts on Adam, who represents humanity, so that Adam, or the humanity embodied in Adam, may put on God. Thus, not only does the baptized attain[33] the pre-fall Adam status,

---

[32] HdPAR VI.9, as provided by S. Brock in "Clothing Metaphors as a Means of Theological Expression in Syriac Tradition" 27.

[33] Perhaps, one should use the phrase "will attain" since, as discussed before, the baptized puts on the robe of glory at baptism but the final fruition of the Paradise status is only attained at the end, at the point of the final resurrection.

but also the status of divinity, which was the intention of God's creation.[34] Thus, one should not view the process of salvation history as merely cyclical; that is, the loss of the robe of glory by Adam and the humanity embodied in him and the regaining of the robe of glory by Adam and the humanity, as the result of the work of the Second Adam, who took on the body of the First Adam to achieve this. Rather, one must view the process as linear. For, the final stage of humankind is perceived as much more glorious than the primordial Paradise; for, God will endow humankind with the divinity, which Adam and Eve attempted to obtain in disobedience to God's command not to eat of the Tree of Life.[35] One can see that the clothing imagery plays a significant role in the Adam typology, which is closely intertwined with the salvation history.

It is more than evident that clothing imagery was integral to Syriac Christian thinking. It is clear in the salvation history, the Adam typology, and isolated sources, all provided above. Yet, it would serve the purposes of this paper to isolate two different types of sources, namely liturgy and hagiography, and discuss the role of clothing language in these sources with the backdrop knowledge of what has been discussed in the previous part of this paper.

The Eucharistic Prayer of Addai and Mari is a liturgical text from the Middle Ages, still in use in some Syriac churches. At this point, a question may

---

[34] S. Brock, "Clothing Metaphors as a Means of Theological Expression in Syriac Tradition" 16.
[35] S. Brock, "Clothing Metaphors as a Means of Theological Expression in Syriac Tradition" 13.

arise. How can one use a text from the Middle Ages to describe the reality of early Syrian Christian experience? Robert Murray affirms such usage based on the static quality of Syriac liturgy and the existence of parallels:

> While it is difficult to use the existing liturgical texts with certainty in discussing the earlier period, since we can know only approximately what the Syriac liturgy and sacramental rites were like in the fourth century, it is permissible to use the liturgical texts for comparison, both because the Syriac Churches have always been very conservative in liturgical matters, and because the authors of the fourth century frequently provide parallels both for features of the existing liturgical texts and for the theology of the sacraments....[36]

This argument deserves a serious consideration.

In light of the general static characteristic of Syriac liturgy, *The Eucharistic Prayer of Addai and Mari* is especially a good liturgical document for examination because A. Gelston prepared this as a critical edition, along with a literary and historical commentary, which attempts to identify the oldest elements in the text, which, Gelston claims, dates around the beginning of the third century, which would make the *Anaphora of Addai and Mari* the

---

[36] 21.

oldest extant anaphora within the Syriac tradition, and most likely the traditional *Anaphora of Edessa*.[37] What is Gelston's argument?

The main argument of Gelston focuses on the lack of an Institution Narrative in the *Anaphora of Addai and Mari* as an evidence for its early dating. His argument hinges on two factors. First, Gelston argues that Syrian Christianity, influenced by Jewish reluctance to fixed prayers, was slow to adopt fixed formulae. Second, the *Anaphora of Addai and Mari* exhibits a common core with the Maronite anaphora *Sharar*, which points to its dating before the Christological debate and the divisions of the fifth century.

Many scholars simply assume that an Institution Narrative was an universal and essential component of early Christian anaphoras. In light of such presumption, they support one of these two theories. First theory argues that an Institution Narrative was inserted in possible nine different places in the *Anaphora of Addai and Mari* when it was liturgically presented. The second theory asserts that the anaphora originally contained an Institution Narrative which was subsequently lost. Gelston, however, stands apart and argues for a third option; that is, the anaphora never contained an Institution Narrative.[38] Gelston refers to Cutrone who states that it is possible that Cyril of Jerusalem's anaphora, in *Cat. Myst.* 5.6-7, moves straight from the *Sanctus* to the *epiklesis* without an Institution Narrative, because,

---

[37]*The Eucharistic Prayer of Addai and Mari* (Oxford: Clarendon Press, 1992) 28.
[38]Gelston 72.

perhaps, it did not contain an Institution Narrative at all. Although Cutrone recognizes other possibilities, perhaps more convincing than one mentioned above, such a possibility obstructs any certain statements to the effect that all anaphoras in the mid-fourth century contained an Institution Narrative.[39] Furthermore, R. P. C. Hanson's powerful article from 1961 establishes that the bishops were at liberty to improvise the text of the Eucharistic Prayer until at least the middle of the third century and argues that the absence of any extant complete liturgies dating before the middle of the fourth century shows that there were few, if any, complete liturgies before the fourth century.[40]

This argument of Hanson points to the influence on Christianity of Jewish hesitation for fixed prayers. After all, first Christians were Jews. Thus, it is not surprising to see early Eucharistic Prayer as influenced by Jewish perception and usage of fixed prayers. Especially lasting was the Jewish influence on Syriac Christianity. A part of the influence can be attested in the participation of Christians of Antioch in the Synagogue worship. John Chrysostom preached against such behavior in 386.[41]

How can one assert that Jews of the post-70 were loath to embrace fixed prayers when one is aware of the *Eighteen Benedictions*? Were they not fixed prayers? This is a point of debate. For, *Berakoth* 4.3-4 indicates that the *Eighteen Benedictions* or the substance of them could be prayed but records Rabbi Eliezer's warning against making a

---

[39] Gelston 75.
[40] Gelston 11.
[41] Gelston 5.

prayer a "fixed task." And in light of TB *Berakoth*, one may perceive "fixed task" as referring to the content, or the formula, rather than to the duty or the regularity of the prayer. TB Berakoth 34a records Eliezer's two disciples who prayed the *Tephillah*, or the *Eighteen Benedictions*. One disciple is recorded as having prayed at great length and the other with great brevity. Such contrast points to the reality that the prayer was not fixed. Furthermore, in 48b-49a, one finds the recording of the need to mention certain items in particular benedictions, but, on the other hand, 29b urges that one say something new in the recitation of the *Tephillah*. This shows that even such a central prayer, as the *Eighteen Benedictions*, had not obtained a fixed formula by the second century.[42] So, there is a certainty that there was an reluctance on the part of the representative mainstream Judaism for fixed prayers. It is more than likely that such attributes made an imprint on the nascent Christian movements. And since Syriac Christianity is the longest Jewish-influenced Christian movement, it is more than likely that there was a reluctance for fixed formulae, like the Institution Narrative.[43]

Another method that Gelston uses to show an early date for the *Anaphora of Addai and Mari* is to identify a common core with the Maronite *Anaphora of Peter III*, otherwise known as *Sharar*. Although these documents represent two separate camps after the separation due to the Christological controversy in the fifth century, the *Anaphora of Addai and Mari*

---

[42]Gelston 4.
[43]Gelston 4.

representing the East Syrians and *Sharar* the Maronites, or the West Syrians, the common core shows that the material predates the Christological controversy and presents itself as not belonging exclusively to the East Syrian tradition.[44]

Section D of the critical text of the *Anaphora of Addai and Mari* shows the closest parallel with *Sharar*, and, therefore, one can assume the material as being very ancient.[45] In fact, Gelston contends that the material belongs to the "oldest stratum of the anaphora."[46] One can see the significant role that clothing imagery plays within the text. The text is provided below so that one may see the clothing language in the context of the "oldest stratum" of the anaphora:

> And with these heavenly hosts we give thee thanks, O my Lord, we also thy unworthy, frail, and miserable servants,
> because thou hast dealt very graciously with us in a way which cannot be repaid,
> in that thou didst assume[47] our humanity that thou mightest restore us to life by thy divinity, and didst exalt our low estate, and raise up our fallen state, and resurrect our mortality, and forgive our sins, and acquit our sinfulness, and enlighten our understanding, and, our Lord and God, overcome our adversaries, and give vic-

---

[44] Gelston 28.
[45] Gelston 90.
[46] Gelston 92.
[47] literally, "clothe thyself with."

tory to the unworthiness of our frail nature in the overflowing mercies of thy grace.[48]

One notices the word "assume" in line 24, which is literally rendered "clothe thyself with," as noted in the note below. One sees that clothing imagery is here employed to describe the incarnation, the stage three of the salvation history. It is interesting to note here what follows in the second part of line 24: "that thou mightest restore us to life by thy divinity." Here, the concept of God taking on humanity so that humanity could take on divinity, discussed under the topic of Adam typology, comes to mind. Thus, one can see that potentially the oldest anaphora in Syriac tradition employed clothing language in an integral way.

    Liturgical expression is not the only way one sees clothing language within Syriac Christianity. Hagiography, perhaps, better shows how deeply ingrained clothing language was within the psyche of the Syrian Christians. For, the purpose of hagiography was not to expound a certain theological concept or to argue a point, but rather to describe, perhaps with some embellishments, what happened to saints and to encourage the readers and listeners toward such model dedication. Therefore, in light of this purpose of hagiography, clothing imagery so firmly rooted in the text stands out blatantly as a firmly ingrained part of the holders of the text; namely, the Syriac Christians.

    In "Mary, Niece of Abraham of Qidun"[49] found in S. Brock and S. Harvey's *Holy Women of the*

---

[48](ed. A. Gelston) lines 21-30.

Syriac Orient, one sees pages colored with clothing imagery. The story recorded in the anthology is an extract from "Life of Abraham of Qidun." This Abraham is a famous fourth century hermit. The earliest Syriac manuscript is from the fifth or sixth century and is anonymous.[50]

Basic summary of the story goes thus. Abraham of Qidun took in Mary, his niece, like his own child when her parents passed away. She lived in the outer part of his house, whereas he, as a recluse, lived in the inner part of the house. She tended to his needs and received spiritual counsel from him. One day, a nominal monk succeeded in seducing Mary into having sexual intercourse with him. Realizing the spiritual consequences of her action which basically undid her whole life of purity, Mary left Abraham's house and became a prostitute. Abraham, realizing her absence, pursued her. He found her finally in a tavern. He disguised himself as a soldier in order to escape her notice so that he would not frighten her before he seized the opportunity to win her back to the way of the righteous. After he was alone with her, he revealed his identity, encouraged her to come back to holy living by assuring her that he would personally take upon himself her guilt. Persuaded, Mary returned with her uncle and remained penitent rest of her days.

The text, although not in entirety and in an edited form, is included in the appendix at the end of this paper. It would serve the purpose of this paper to point out and discuss clothing imagery painted

---

[49]Brock and Harvey 29-36.
[50]Brock and Harvey 27.

throughout the account. When Mary committed fornication and realized the import of what she had done, the text describes: "she tore off the garment she was wearing" (paragraph 18). In the same paragraph, Mary exclaims in the text: "I have wrapped myself in shame by becoming a laughing stock to the Enemy, Satan." In the next paragraph, one reads: "She changed the precious monastic garb she had been wearing and established herself in a low tavern." One cannot help but notice that clothing imagery for Mary is here used in parallel to the fall of Adam and Eve. Mary had a pure, monastic robe, symbolic of the robe of glory with which Adam and Eve were originally clothed. In the same manner in which Adam and Eve lost their robes of glory after the fall, Mary gives up her monastic robe. As Adam and Eve were covered in fig leaves, Mary considers herself covered in shame. And just as Adam and Eve "fell from grace" and were physically moved out of the Paradise into cursed land, Mary moves from the house of her uncle Abraham which represents a sort of a paradise[51] and into a "low tavern," surrounded by sin. Thus, using the language of salvation history,

---

[51] One notices that the text described the house as having two parts: the inner part where Abraham stayed and the outer part where Mary stayed. One questions whether this was intentionally written on the part of the author as a metaphor for the Jerusalem temple which also was divided into two parts, with the inner part being the holy of holies. If the house represents the temple, a sort of a paradise or a picture of the paradise, and at the least the agency through which one may gain entrance to the paradise, then going away from it is certainly a picture of expulsion from the paradise.

one may describe Mary's sin and her leaving the paradise as representing scenes one and two.

Clothing imagery is not merely confined to Mary. In the episodes that concern Abraham's rescue of Mary one clearly sees the employment of clothing language. Two years of seeking information for Mary's whereabouts brought fruit and, as a result, Abraham sets out for the tavern in which Mary had her stay for two years. But before he sets out, the text describes that "the blessed man asked to have brought to him an outfit of soldier's clothing" (paragraph 20). Later in the paragraph, one sees Abraham's intention for such a request. He wanted to escape detection. The text reads: "He put on the military dress with a helmet on his head so that his face was covered." Again in the same paragraph, one finds the description of Abraham as "wearing the local dress to prevent detection: thus did the blessed man wear those clothes whereby he could overcome the Adversary." Although one finds Abraham's soldier-wear as representing his preparation to conquer Satan, called here, "the Adversary," the stronger motif is surely the concept of hiding his own identity. His identity is covered by local outfit so that local people would not recognize him, the venerable saint Abraham. This story of one hiding one's true identity in order to mingle within a group of people surely reminds one of the third stage of salvation history, namely the incarnation of the Word. Divinity took upon himself a body so that he might dwell among those with bodies, robbed of robes of glory, in order that he might affect salvation of humankind at the point of baptism, in which he made it possible for humanity to regain the robe of glory by means of his own baptism. So incarnation had as its motif also a concept of divinity being covered with something that would make him fit in with the "local" people. Thus, one may describe Abraham of the story as a type of Christ. And, indeed, Abraham does go to a place of sin, the tavern, where Mary was employed as a hostess-prostitute. Resemblance to Jesus of Nazareth's "open table fellowship" [52] is evident in paragraph 22, in which the narrator, in an amazed tone, describes Abraham's actions:

> What wisdom of spirit, what true discernment in the company he kept! This man, who for fifty years had not even eaten any bread due to his ascetic way of life, now, for the sake of one soul, ate meat and drank wine, all in order to rescue a lost soul. The angle hosts stood in astonishment at the blessed man's discerning action, how with a good will and without any hesitation, he ate and drank, all in order to draw up a soul that had sunk into foul-smelling mire. How great is the wisdom of the truly wise, what perception do those who truly understand possess!

---

[52] "Open table fellowship" refers to the practice of Jesus of Nazareth in which he associated with and ate at the same table with social outcasts and the ritually impure, referred to in the Gospels as "publicans and sinners." Such individuals included prostitutes, people with leprosy, and tax collectors.

The narrator's enthusiasm for Abraham must be seen in light of his identity as a type of Christ. Even in the context of this passage, the image of Christ as the Good Shepherd who values even one lost soul is expressed in Abraham's person. What many would perceive as not holy, Abraham did in order to save one soul. This surely reminds one of the Gospel accounts' portrayal of Jesus of Nazareth. Just as the soteriological work of Jesus is portrayed in Syriac Christian thought in clothing language, the rescue process of Abraham, a type of Christ, is portrayed in clothing imagery, reminiscent of Jesus' work.

Abraham's identity is revealed only at the point of Mary's salvation from her newly acquired filthy life. When Abraham was alone in the room with Mary, he grabbed her firmly and "he removed his helmet from his head" (paragraph 24). One sees clothing language in his revelation of himself. Also, when Abraham desires to save Mary, he utilizes clothing language to rebuke her and remind her of the glorious past. Abraham says: "Where is that precious monastic habit you used to wear?" (paragraph 24). Implicit here is the notion that she needs to wear her previous "monastic habit" again. Here, the understanding of salvation in Syriac Christianity as gaining back the robe of glory comes to mind. Mary now needs to gain back her robe of glory.

Thus, Mary's repentance is seen as leaving behind "clothes" that she acquired in her sinful life along with the money acquired in the same way. Abraham urged her to abandon them when she asked him: "There's a little gold and a lot of clothes that I've picked up in the course of my life of shame, what should I do with them?" (paragraph 24). One notices the emphasis on clothes. This is in keeping with Syriac Christianity's propensity to attach symbolic significance to clothes and clothing language.

The story closes with Mary repentant and "dressed in sackcloth and humility" (paragraph 25). She prays in repentance, fasts, keeps vigil by night. Even in her prayer, called the "Lament of Mary," Mary uses clothing imagery to describe how she fell from a place of honor into sin:

> GOMAL He removed from my countenance the honorable veil -- alas is me! He made me live, shamefaced, in a tavern. Fie on you, Evil One; what is it you have wrought in me?

It is more than clear that clothing imagery plays a foundational role in the psyche of Syriac Christians to the extent that their hagiography, stories about saints which are not theological treatises, is even colored with clothing language.

Syriac Christianity, the strand of Christianity most influenced by Jewish thought and interpretation, embraced parallel interpretation of Genesis 3:21, that emphasized the loss of the robe of glory at the Fall, rather than the traditional "Graeco-Roman" Christianity's emphasis on the covering of nakedness at the Fall. Syriac Christian theology came to be focused on the loss of this robe of glory by the First Adam and the need to regain this lost robe of glory. This retrieval is perceived as salvation and the agent of redemption is the incarnate Word, or the Second

Adam. Thus, in Brock's four-scene salvation history in the Syriac Christian thinking, one sees the integral role clothing symbolism plays in each scene. First scene, the creation, portrays Adam and Eve dressed in robes of glory; scene two, the Fall, shows them stripped of their robe of glory. Scene three, the incarnation of the Word, shows divinity taking on a body, the body of the First Adam, in order to bring about salvation, seen as regaining of the lost robe of glory. Scene four, the baptism of Jesus, shows that Jesus left the robe of glory in the sacral baptismal water, so that all who are baptized may pick up the robe of glory and look toward the eschatological paradise, in which they will achieve perfection to the extent of divinity. Adam typology, as one can see, plays a significant role, especially because humanity is embodied in the First Adam. Sources provided in the discussion of the four-scene salvation history and the Adam typology show the integral role of clothing imagery. But one notices how far-reaching this imagery is when one views the *Anaphora of Addai and Mari*, a liturgical text still in use, today. Although one identifies the oldest element, which contains clothing imagery, as belonging to the third or the fourth century, the liturgical expression remains timeless within Syriac Christianity. Furthermore, the deep influence of clothing imagery in Syriac tradition is attested in the intricate and crucial role it plays within hagiography, especially in the account, "Mary, Niece of Abraham of Qidun," which received much attention and discussion in this paper. This is especially significant in light of the fact that hagiography does not have as its primary purpose theological didaction, rather its main purpose is to provide examples to follow and to preserve accounts of saints. Thus, such integral role of clothing imagery in "Mary, Niece of Abraham of Qidun," along with parallelism with four-scene salvation history and Christ-typology of Abraham of Qidun, point to the deep-rootedness of clothing imagery in the psyche of Syriac Christianity.

APPENDIX 1: Edited "Mary, Niece of Abraham of Qidun"

"When these twenty years had elapsed, Satan took notice of her and tried to ensnare her; his intention was to cause the blessed Abraham grief and pain by these means, thus diverting his mind from God. Now there was a man who was nominally a monk, who used regularly to come and visit the blessed Abraham on the pretext of friendship. One day he happened to see the blessed girl through the window. He fell in love with her at the mere sight and wanted to get hold of her and sleep with her. .... For a whole year he treacherously lay in wait for her, until he succeeded in softening her firm resolve, and the girl eventually opened the door of the house where she lived as a recluse and came out to see him. He assaulted her with his blandishments, bespattering her with the mud of his lust. Once this sinful episode had taken place, stupefaction seized hold of her mind: *she tore off the garment she was wearing*, beat her face and breasts in grief, and said to herself, 'I am now as good as dead: I have lost all the days of my life; my ascetic labors, my abstinence, my tears are all wasted, for I have rebelled against God and slain my soul; and upon my holy uncle I have imposed bitter grief. *I have wrapped myself in shame* by becoming a laughing stock to the Enemy, Satan. .... What has become of this saintly man's instruction, what has happened to the wise Ephrem's warnings? They told me to be careful of myself and preserve my virginity spotless for the immortal Bridegroom. 'Your bridegroom is holy and jealous,' they said. .... So straightaway she got up and left for another town. *She changed the precious monastic garb she had been wearing* and established for herself in a low tavern. After this had taken place, the blessed Abraham had a fearful vivid dream: he beheld a huge serpent, disgusting to look at and hissing in a fearsome way. On leaving its lair it came toward him; it found there a dove, swallowed it up, and went back to its lair. .... Then once again, two days later, he saw the same serpent leave its lair and come toward his house, whereupon it placed its head beneath the blessed man's feet; the serpent's belly was then ripped open, and there, safe and sound in its belly was the dove that it had swallowed. The blessed man stretched out his hand and took the dove, which was still alive and unharmed. On waking up he called to the blessed girl once and then a second time, saying, 'My daughter, why are you so negligent: for two days you have not opened your mouth to praise God.' Seeing that she did not answer, and that for two days she had not ministered to his needs as was her wont, the blessed man realized that the dream he had seen referred to her. He groaned and wept plenteously, saying, 'Alas for my lamb, the wolf has snatched her away; my daughter has been taken captive.' .... Now the two days between the blessed man's two dreams represented the years during which his niece lived in the world. ..... After two years the blessed man discovered where she was living. ... *the blessed man asked to have brought to him an outfit of soldier's clothing* and a horse. When these arrived, he opened the door of his home and came out. *He put on the military dress with a helmet on his head so that his face was covered,* mounted the horse, and set off -- like a spy wanting to scout out some region or town, *wearing the local dress to prevent detection*: *thus did the blessed man wear those clothes whereby he could overcome the Adversary.* .... When he arrived at the spot ... he spoke to the tavern keeper with a smile on his lips, 'My friend, I've heard you have a pretty lass here; I'd like to see her.' .... This man, who for fifty years had not even eaten any bread due to his ascetic way of life, now, for the sake of one soul, ate meat and drank wine, all in order to rescue a lost soul. The angel hosts stood in astonishment at the blessed man's discerning action, how with a good will and without any hesitation, he ate and drank, all in order to draw up a soul that had sunk into foul-smelling mire. .... After they had chatted together, the girl said, 'Please come into my bedroom so that we can sleep together.' .... On entering he espied a large bed made up, and of his own accord he sat down beside her. .... So she shut the door and came back to him. ...he grasped her firmly to prevent her escaping and ... *he removed his helmet from his head* and spoke to her with tears in his eyes: '.... What has happened to you, my daughter? Who has killed you this way -- or so it seems? *Where is that precious monastic habit you used to wear?* ....' .... 'My daughter, I have taken upon myself your

wrongdoing: God will require this sin at my hands. ....' ....
'There's a little gold and a lot of clothes that I've picked up in the course of my life of shame, what should I do with them?' she asked. 'Leave them all here; they belong to the Evil One,' he said. .... When they arrived, he enclosed her in the inner part of the house where he had previously lived, while he took up residence in the outer part, which had formerly been her place. *Dressed in sackcloth and humility*, she spent her time in tears and vigil, fasting and showing great diligence in her penitence as, without any hesitation, she called upon God who has pity on sinners. Her repentance was completely sincere. ...."[53] (ed. S. Brock and A. Harvey) paragraphs 18-25.

---

[53]Italics Mine. They refer to clothing imagery within the narrative.

Bibliography

Brock, Sebastian P. "Clothing Metaphors as a Means of Theological Expression in Syriac Tradition." *Typus, Symbol, Allegorie beiden östlichen Vätern und ihren Parallelen im Mittelalter.* Ed. M. Schmidt and C. F. Geyer. Regensburg: Verlag Friedrich Pustet, 1982, 11-38.

Brock, Sebastian P. "Early Syriac Asceticism." *Numen* XX (1973) 1-19.

Brock, Sebastian P. "Greek into Syriac and Syriac into Greek." *Journal of the Syriac Academy* III (1977) 422-406.

Brock, Sebastian P. "Jewish Traditions in Syriac Sources." *Journal of Jewish Studies* XXX (1979) 212-232.

Brock, Sebastian P., and Susan A. Harvey. *Holy Women of the Syrian Orient.* Berkeley and Los Angeles: University of California Press, 1987.

Gärtner, Bertil. *The Temple and the Community in Qumran and the New Testament.* Cambridge: At the University Press, 1965.

Gelston, A. *The Eucharistic Prayer of Addai and Mari*. Oxford: Clarendon Press, 1992.

Murray, Robert. *Symbols of Church and Kingdom: A Study in Early Syriac Tradition*. Cambridge: Cambridge University Press, 1975.

Rouwhorst, G. A. M. *Les Hymnes Pascales d'Ephrem de Nisibe (I: Etude)*. Leiden: E. J. Brill, 1989.

Rouwhorst, G. A. M. *Les Hymnes Pascales d'Ephrem de Nisibe (II: Textes)*. Leiden: E. J. Brill, 1989.

"Marriage in the Qumran Community"[1]

Based on Jewish authors from the first century of the Common Era, many scholars have held the existence of hostility toward marriage in the Qumran community as a truism. This perception, however, is faulty in light of several considerations. First of all, the very existence of marriage laws points to a concern about marriage. Second of all, a realist tendency in Qumran laws in general, and in Qumran marriage laws in particular, shows emphasis on "nature." This very reality points to a positive perception of marriage, understood as a natural institution created by God.

Both Philo and Josephus depict the Essenes as rejecting marriage, although Josephus interjects that there was a subgroup of Essenes who valued marriage for the purpose of propagation of the race, the "chief function of life."[2] Identifying the Qumran community as a subgroup of the Essenes, many scholars have ascribed such attitude as germane to the Qumran community. Geza Vermes is a scholar who holds to that perspective; he argues that the

---

[1] This paper was written in Jerusalem, Israel, in 1994. I would like to acknowledge the generosity of The Goldsmith Foundation and the State of Israel for funding my research stay at the Hebrew University of Jerusalem as a Visiting Research Fellow. I would like also to thank Professor Daniel Schwartz of the Jewish History Department at the Hebrew University of Jerusalem who read the complete draft of the paper and gave many helpful comments.
[2] Josephus, *War* 2.160.

Qumran community was exclusively a celibate-male society. Furthermore, quoting 1QS 1:6 - DSSE 72³, Vermes argues that the Qumran "sectaries" had a hostile attitude toward sex and marriage. Vermes also notes that the word *ishah*, woman, is found only once in the *Community Rule* in a peripheral manner, which, in Vermes' mind, enforces the argument for celibacy within the Qumran community.⁴ As much as Vermes would like to believe that "few will probably disagree that the idea of the presence of women among them appears incongruous,"⁵ his position is not uniformly accepted. Joseph Baumgarten voices dissent. For Baumgarten, although ancient Jewish writers, such as Philo and Josephus, perceived celibacy as a major tenet in the Essene faith, Qumran writings offer a contrary picture of the perception of marriage by the Qumran community. Baumgarten argues that both the *Damascus Document* (CD) and the *Temple Scroll* (11QT) contain sectarian rules concerning marriage. Furthermore, the *Messianic Rule* (1QSa), according to Baumgarten, takes marriage as a normal step in the maturation of a young man. Baumgarten, also, presents the Cave 4 text (4Q502), which praises women possessing qualities of "intelligence and understanding," as a support for the integral role women played in the communal life of the Qumran community.⁶

---

³"not to follow a sinful heart and lustful eyes, committing all manner of evil"
⁴Geza Vermes, *The Dead Sea Scrolls: Qumran in Perspective* (Philadelphia: Fortress Press, 1977) 96-97.
⁵Vermes 96.
⁶ Joseph Baumgarten, "The Qumran-Essene Restraints on Marriage" in *Archaeology and History in the Dead Sea Scrolls*

The existence of marriage laws among the Qumran sources cannot be gainsaid. For instance, in *Damascus Document* 4:20-21, one finds a prohibition against a man marrying two times in his life time, if one takes the text literally. There have been debates concerning this text. The point of disagreement is whether the text should be taken as it is found or if one should note a scribal error within the text. Jerome Murphy-O'Connor takes the text literally. Yigael Yadin disagrees and claims a scribal error in the text. Yadin claims that the prohibition is for a man marrying again in her, his wife's, life time. Yadin cites column 57:17-19[7] of the *Temple Scroll* to support his claim.[8] The reason for concern over detail is that interpretation carries greater significance in one's understanding of the Qumran perspective on polygamy and divorce. If one takes the prohibition as being of a man taking two wives in his life time, the implication is that he may not marry another, whether she is dead or even if he divorces her. If one

---

(ed. Lawrence Schiffman) (Sheffield: JSOT Press, 1990, pp. 13-24) 13-14.

[7] Yigael Yadin provides his translation of the text: "Et il ne prendra pas en plus d'elle (la première femme dont il est question précédement) une autre femme, car elle seule sera avec lui tous les jours de sa vie; et si elle meurt, il prendra pour lui-même une autre (femme)."

[8] As Professor Daniel Schwartz noted in a personal discussion, Leviticus 18:18 shows the biblical precedent for the Hebrew word in question. Leviticus 18:18 states: "Do not take your wife's sister as a rival wife and have sexual relations with her while *your wife is living*" (Italics Mine). The Hebrew word for the italics is the same word (in singular) of the word that Yigael Yadin claims should be in the Qumran text. This biblical precedent strengthens Yadin's claim.

takes the prohibition as being of a man taking two wives in her life time, the implication is a prohibition of polygamy and alludes to restriction on divorce. And accordingly, both Murphy-O'Connor and Yigael Yadin stand by these implications of their translations of the text.[9] These scholars wrestled with the interpretation of a Qumran marriage law, but underneath their efforts is the premise that this marriage law belonged to the Qumran document. At this juncture, one may ask the rhetorical question: if marriage was seen as a negative thing in the Qumran community, why was there a law concerning correct behavior vis-a-vis marriage?

Another marriage law found in the Qumran community concerns marriage with nieces. *Damascus Document* 4 complains that sinners marry their nieces. The Qumran document applies Leviticus 18:13 to women. Leviticus 18:13 states: "Do not have sexual relations with your mother's sister, because she is your mother's close relative" (NIV). Thus, just as nephews must not marry, nor have sexual relations with, their aunts, nieces must not marry, nor have sexual relations with, their uncles.[10] This position stands in stark contrast to the nominalist approach of the rabbinical law. There is no such prohibition in the rabbinical law. Presumed under the nominalist rabbinical position is the idea

---

[9]Yigael Yadin, "L'attitude essénienne envers la polygamie et le divorce" in *Revue biblique* (Volume 79, 1972, pp. 98-99) 98-99.
[10]Daniel Schwartz, "Law and Truth: On Qumran-Sadducean and Rabbinic View of Law" in *The Dead Sea Scrolls: Forty Years of Research* (ed. Devorah Dimant and Uriel Rapport) (Leiden: E. J. Brill, 1992, pp. 229-240) 231.

that what is not forbidden explicitly in the Torah is allowed. But operating from the realist perspective, the Qumran community applied the principles of Torah in light of present reality. Thus, interdict against males marrying one relation horizontal and then one relation vertical would apply both upwards and downwards.

This realist tendency in the Qumran law regarding marriage with nieces is congruous with the larger Qumran legal corpus. An example is found in the question regarding ritual purity of animal bones. Numbers 19:16c states: "anyone who touches a human bone or a grave, will be unclean for seven days" (NIV). For a nominalist, human bone is unclean because the law states that it is unclean. One finds this thought in the rabbinical tradition. But for the realist, human bone is impure because bones are impure. Thus, in contrast to the rabbinical tradition, the *Temple Scroll* (LI) shows that the Qumran community believed animal bones to be impure as well, although such statement is not found in the Torah. After all, it is inconceivable for a realist to admit that the superior human bone is impure while the inferior animal bone is pure.[11]

Another example of a realist tendency in Qumran law is found in penal law. Deuteronomy 17:6 states: "On the testimony of two or three witnesses a man shall be put to death, but no one shall be

---

[11]Schwartz 232. In his articles, Professor Schwartz also notes a similarity between the Qumran realists and the Sadducees. According to the Mishnaic report of the position of the "Sadducees" on *Yadaim* 4:7, the Sadducees viewed animal bones as sources of impurity as well.

put to death on the testimony of only one witness" (NIV). The rabbinical tradition shows its nominalist content by upholding the letter of the law. If there are not two or three witnesses to a single crime, the accused may go free, even if it is obvious that the person committed the crime or even if he had a history of such accusations. For the Qumran realists, this was not acceptable. If a person had a series of such accusations or if it was obvious that he had committed the crime, it defeats the spirit of the law for such person to go free. No doubt, Deuteronomy 17:6 was meant to protect the falsely accused, but its purpose was not to let a guilty go, when it was clear that he was guilty. Thus, the Qumran realists interpreted this law as requiring two witnesses together for a single crime or three witnesses separately for different crimes of penal nature. Either group of witnesses would suffice to convict a person (CD 9:16-22).[12] This case shows that the Qumran realists were concerned with what was actually the case, rather than what was legally culpable.

On account of the realist position of Qumran law, J. M. Baumgarten, Y. Sussman, B. Z. Wacholder have noted the agreement between Qumran and Sadducean law on various points. Daniel Schwartz takes a step further and forwards the thesis that Qumran realists and the Sadducees had common roots[13]

---

[12]Schwartz 233.

[13]Louis Ginsberg in his *An Unknown Jewish Sect* notes that the original sectarians in Judea originated from the Pharisees and not from the Sadducees (New York: The Jewish Theological Seminary of America, 1976, p. 267). In fact, Ginsberg's efforts to show congruence of the *Damascus Document* to rabbinical halakah is praiseworthy. And, one cannot deny the fact that

"in a period before the schism."[14] Because Qumran sectarians had priestly roots, they attacked the Wicked Priest and the "last priests of Jerusalem" in some of their documents. This would certainly explain the realist tendency in Qumran law. Priests are priests by birth, by an act of nature, a system created by God, so their legitimacy is based on birth, on nature. Such reality would exhibit itself in law and it does.

Pharisees, or rabbis, on the other hand, do not have their legitimacy based on birth; rather, their legitimacy stems from the law, or their expertise in it. Their ability to explain and uphold the law brings them value. Thus, rabbis are dependent on the law. A good example of this is found in *Rosh HaShanah* 2:8-9. Rabban Gamaliel's court mistakenly set the Day of Atonement a day too early, but the rabbis decided to uphold the wrong decision because questioning a decision of the court would compel them to question decisions of every court since Moses' days. The Qumran community would have perceived this as outrageous. For this is tantamount to saying that God's appointed times are those which the court

---

there are similarities between rabbinical law and the *Damascus Document*. For example, there are similarities in concern over ritual observance of the Sabbath. But on the other hand, Ginsberg exerts too much effort to gainsay any sectarianism in the document. Operating from pre-Dead Sea scroll standpoint, his analysis deserves much praise; yet, I find Professor Schwartz's arguments much more insightful in that he examines the nature of various halakah's in terms of nominalism and realism. For Professor Schwartz's analysis reaches into the heart of legal interpretation and does not merely make surface comparisons.
[14]Schwartz 229.

pronounces.[15] But the behavior of the rabbis is understandable, because their authority derives from their interpretation and upholding of the law. To say their decision in a matter is wrong is essentially undermining their only means of practicing power.

The Qumran sectarians, on the contrary, operated from a realist perspective, because their legitimacy was biologically based. This is evident in their argument for monogamy. *Damascus Document 4* gives an argument from creation found in Genesis 1:27c[16] as a support for monogamy. Genesis 1:27c

---

[15] Schwartz 234. The Qumran community utilized the solar calendar, whereas the Pharisees used the lunar calendar. Thus, festival dates were set for the Qumran community, but the Pharisees had to determine the sacred days. Schwartz comments on the Qumran position: "That is to say, festivals have their set times, according to the movement of the heavenly bodies which God ordained and fixed, and it is man's job to discover and observe them, not to determine them" (235).

[16] It is interesting to note here that Jesus of Nazareth also used this argument from creation in his teaching on marriage and divorce. Jesus' saying concerning divorce is multiply attested in Matthew 5:31-32; Matthew 19:3-12; Mark 10:2-12; Luke 16:18; and I Corinthians 7:10-11 {here, Paul of Tarsus states "To the married I give this command (not I, but the Lord)" (NIV)}. And in two of the passages listed above, Jesus is quoted as having used Genesis 1:27c as an argument against divorce. Matthew 19:4-6 reads: "'Haven't you read,' he [Jesus] replied, 'that at the beginning the Creator "made them male and female," and said, "For this reason a man will leave his father and mother and be united to his wife and the two will become one flesh"? So they are no longer two, but one. Therefore what God has joined together, let man not separate'" (NIV). In the parallel passage found in Mark 10:6-9, Jesus is quoted as having said: "But at the beginning of creation God 'made them male and female.' 'For this reason a man will leave his father and mother and be united to his wife, and the two will become one flesh.' So they

reads: "male and female he created them" (NIV). The reason why one should have a monogamous marriage is not because there is a Mosaic law circumscribing it. Rather, it was meant to be; it was a part of nature, which God instituted. In *Damascus*

---

are no longer two, but one. Therefore what God has joined together, let man not separate" (NIV). From passages quoted above, one can see that Jesus is shown to have taught monogamy. This is grounded in the creation principle quoted from Genesis 1:27. Furthermore, based on the same Genesis passage, Jesus of Nazareth is shown to have looked unfavorably upon divorce. In both passages, Jesus tells the Pharisees that the only reason why Moses allowed for a certification of divorce is that human hearts were hardened (Matthew 19:7f.; Mark 10:3f.). It is not surprising to see Jesus of Nazareth describing the Mosaic Law as the alternative to the creation norm. In other parts of the Christian canon, one can also find the practice of Jesus setting his authority over that of the Mosaic Law. The Sermon on the Mount (Matthew 5-7) provides such an example. For instance, Jesus of Nazareth is quoted as saying: "You have heard that it was said, 'Do not commit adultery.' But I tell you that anyone who looks at a woman lustfully has already committed adultery with her in his heart" (Matthew 5:27f. NIV). Now, one may ask: Does Jesus' teaching on divorce using the creation argument show a Qumran influence? On the surface, the answer may seem to be a simple "yes." But one needs to consider the element of Jesus denigrating the Mosaic Law. No one in Qumran would have dared to describe the Mosaic Law in such pejorative manner. Thus, according to the criterion of coherence, Jesus' teaching on divorce belongs to *Sitz im Leben* 1. (The criterion of coherence can be seen in this manner: when a saying of Jesus of Nazareth described in one part of the Christian canon is congruous with his teaching and action throughout the canon, then it may be assumed to belong originally to Jesus of Nazareth.) Whether Jesus was aware of the Qumran sources and utilized its sources to fit his agenda cannot be answered within the confines of this paper. It is possible, but most likely improbable.

Document 5, the author goes on further to support his argument stemming from Nature by noting that those who entered the ark entered in two's. This is significant because, according to the biblical account of the flood, everything and everyone outside of the ark perished with the flood. Only those who were in the ark survived the disaster. The underlying presupposition behind the author's use of this content to support his argument for monogamy is the idea that just as God created one male for one female, the way of nature is for one male living thing to be in a sexual union with one female living thing. In other words, a man should be married with a woman. This is how God meant things to be.

The realist tendency in Qumran law stands stark in the author's defense of David, who had more than one wife. In book five of the *Damascus Document*, the author justifies David's action by stating that David had not read the sealed book of the *Law* that was in the ark of the Covenant; for, the sealed book was not opened from the death of Eleazar and Joshua until the coming of Zadok. It is important to note that the author considered his arguments for monogamy derived from arguments based on nature as being part of the Law. Of course, one refers to the first five books of the Hebrew Scriptures as the Law, or Torah, but the reasons that the author provided were not what would be clearly seen as Law. For the Law was given to Moses on Mount Sinai. Thus, when one refers to the Law, one thinks of Deuteronomy or Leviticus. This was certainly the case with the Pharisees, who did not perceive polygamy as being opposed to the Mosaic Law. After all, there was no clear legal prohibition against polygamy. Furthermore, men of great faith in the Scriptures had more than one wife. But for the Qumran sectarians, it was not natural. A realist outlook demanded emphasis on monogamy. Why would God create only one woman for one man if it was not the way God intended for marriage? The Qumran community, therefore, not only had laws regarding marriage, it was careful to outline how that marriage should be. The Qumran community applied realist legal perspective to marriage and perceived monogamy as the legal norm and the natural thing to do. In book four of the *Damascus Document*, marrying another woman while being married to one wife is seen as fornication. Such careful attention to detail regarding marriage surely points to the existence of marriage within the community, or at least to a positive perception of marriage as a natural thing to do.

In fact, one finds in the *Rule of the Congregation* (1QSa) 1:10-11 a mention of age twenty as the minimum age for marriage and starting of a family. According to 4Q*Ordinance* 2:6-9, this is the only time that the sectarian is supposed to contribute the half shekel donation to the temple. Based on this information, Lawrence Schiffman argues that a member of the Qumran sect remains under the authority of his family until he is granted a full status as a member at the age of twenty along with anyone attached to him by marriage -- such as a wife and children. According to Schiffman, a woman not born into the sect may obtain membership merely upon marriage.[17] Thus, marriage is seen as a normal step in the stage of the sectarian life.

In order to show that marriage was a normal stage in the life of the Qumran sectarian, Lawrence Schiffman argues against commonly held exegesis of the passage found in the *Rule of the Congregation* (1QSa) 2:3-11, which reads: "And any man who is afflicted [with any one of] the human uncleanness shall not enter into the congregation of these." Some scholars have taken this passage as indicative of a prohibition on marriage. Schiffman, on the other hand, asserts that Lamentations 1:10 in conjunction with the larger context in which the text is found shows this passage to be a prohibition on entry into the Israelite *sancta*, "represented by the temple in lamentations and the sectarian eschatological assembly in our passage."[18] Lamentations 1:10 reads: "The enemy laid hands on all her treasures; she saw pagan nations enter her sanctuary -- those you had forbidden to enter your assembly" (NIV). Here, one can see that "congregation" or "assembly" is seen as "sanctuary." Schiffman's argument is stronger than those of his opponents especially because those who claim that the Qumran community was hostile to marriage posit that the Qumran community perceived women negatively.[19] But how strong is this argument for misogyny in the Qumran community?

---

[17]Lawrence Schiffman, *The Eschatological Community of the Dead Sea Scrolls: A Study of the Rule of the Congregation* (Atlanta: Scholars Press, 1989) 18.
[18]Schiffman 37.
[19]Some prohibitions for ritual purity may be construed as a prohibition against women. But this is not necessarily the case. For instance, 11QT45 extends the period of defilement after

The Cave 4 text (4Q502) provides a resounding "no" to the question above. The text praises women possessing characteristics of "intelligence and understanding" as "daughters of truth" and "sisters" within the *yahad*. This passage demonstrates that women functioned as an integral part of the Qumran community. Furthermore, there is a positive allusion to "a man and his wife" in the Cave 4 text. The positive perception of women would certainly be congruous with the burial of women and children in the Qumran cemetery.[20]

Thus, Joseph Baumgarten explains Josephus' *War* 2:161 in light of the Cave 4 text. In this passage, there is a mention of a three year premarital probationary period for women who wanted to marry an Essene. Baumgarten rejects the notion that this probationary period was for the purpose of assessing whether or not the menstrual cycle was regular. Demonstration of character, rather than anything physical, was the issue. The fact that the probationary period for women was equal to that of the novice before his full admission into the community supports this argument. Furthermore, Baumgarten

---

intercourse to three days as against one day, as it is outlined in the Pentateuchal law (Leviticus 15:18). This is not because the Qumran community had a more negative view on women, but rather this may be understood in light of the perception in the Qumran community that revelation was still an ongoing process. Thus, it wanted to observe ritual purity in the same manner as that for the receiving of the revelation at Mount Sinai years before (Baumgarten 19-20).

[20] Baumgarten 13-14. Baumgarten, however, questions Lawrence Schiffman's interpretation of the joyous celebration in the Cave 4 text as a marriage ritual.

posits that support for this argument is provided by the fact that "the identical verb *dokimazo* [is] employed by Josephus to denote the demonstration of character compatible with the discipline of the order."[21] Indeed, in light of the Cave 4 text, which shows value of moral traits in women, Baumgarten's argument stands strong.

Thus, it is clear that there was no misogyny or hostility toward marriage in the Qumran community. Not only do Qumran documents discuss proper marriage in careful detail, but the realist tendency in Qumran law in general and Qumran marriage laws in particular also opposes a hostile sentiment toward marriage. After all, God made them "male and female." Marriage is a natural institution established by God. To say that it was wrong would be tantamount to stating that God made a mistake.

---

[21]Baumgarten 16.

Bibliography

Baumgarten, Joseph. "The Qumran-Essene Restraints on Marriage." *Archaeology and History in the Dead Sea Scrolls*. Ed. Lawrence Schiffman. Sheffield: JSOT Press, 1990. Pages 13-24.

Ginsberg, Louis. *An Unknown Jewish Sect*. New York: The Jewish Theological Seminary of America, 1976.

Schiffman, Lawrence. *The Eschatological Community of the Dead Sea Scrolls: A Study of the Rule of the Congregation*. Atlanta: Scholars Press, 1989.

Schwartz, Daniel. "Law and Truth: On Qumran-Sadducean and Rabbinic View of Law." *The Dead Sea Scrolls: Forty Years of Research*. Ed. Devorah Dimant and Uriel Rapport. Leiden: E. J. Brill, 1992. Pages 229-240.

Vermes, Geza. *The Dead Sea Scrolls: Qumran in Perspective*. Philadelphia: Fortress Press, 1977.

Yadin, Yigael. "L'attitude essénienne envers la polygamie et le divorce." *Revue biblique*. Volume 79: 1972. Pages 98-99.

Heerak Christian Kim

"Philo of Alexandria's Portrait of Moses"[1]

Philo of Alexandria greatly respected Moses. Thus, Philo felt especially compelled to give an account of Moses' life so that others might know him through his characteristics and life's story and not merely through the Mosaic Law. Philo carefully expounds on four roles of Moses: philosopher-king, legislator, priest, and prophet. From birth and throughout his life, Moses is depicted by Philo as being unique. In fact, he is almost "the perfect man" to Philo.

But before Philo actually starts his depiction of Moses, he first legitimizes his writing. Philo feels that he is "more accurately acquainted than other people"[2] concerning the life of Moses from the Scriptures and Jewish elders. This could be seen as a kind of citing more authoritative works in proof of his writings. This practice can be found in other writings of his times. The New Testament writings have frequent referral to the Hebrew Scriptures. For example, Mark writes, "It is written in Isaiah the Prophet,"[3] referring back to a revered prophet who would give legitimacy to his writing. The short introduction in the first few lines in which Philo

---

[1] I would like to thank Professor Michael A. Signer, the Director of Notre Dame University Holocaust Project, for his helpful comments on the paper and his many positive encouragements.
[2] Philo Judaeus, "On the Life of Moses," <u>The Essential Philo</u>, ed. Nahum N. Glatzer (New York: Schocken Books, 1971, pp. 190-270) 192.
[3] Mark 1:2, The New International Version

places the defense of his writing raises the question of the audience that Philo is addressing. Some scholars believe that he is addressing a Gentile audience to show, in an apologetic way, the superiority of the Jewish law and the lawgiver Moses. One such scholar is Émile Bréhier of the Sorbonne, and he writes, "Le Moïse est une œvre apologétique adressée aux païens pour montrer la supériorité du législateur juif et de sa législation sur tous les autres."[4] Erwin R. Goodenough takes a step further and claims that Philo's writing On the Life of Moses went beyond mere apologetics; Goodenough feels that it was an effort at converting gentiles.[5] But, Samuel Sandmel strongly disagrees with Goodenough and also with Bréhier for that matter. Sandmel feels that because Gentiles did not read Jewish writings, the only possibility is that Philo, with a conversionist purpose, was addressing Jews in Alexandria who were on the point of leaving the Jewish faith, like Philo's nephew. Thus, Sandmel strongly criticizes Goodenough with these words: "...the supposition that the direct purpose of On Moses was to convert Gentiles seems a bit extreme."[6] One may indeed say that the theory about the conversion of Gentiles "seems a bit extreme." But, on the other hand, the theory about the conversion of Jews in Alexandria also "seems a bit extreme." For, even with the supposition that

---

[4] Émile Bréhier, Les Idées Philosophiques et Religieuses de Philon d'Alexandrie (Paris: Librairie Philosophique J. Vrin, 1950) 7.
[5] Samuel Sandmel, Philo of Alexandria: An Introduction (New York: Oxford University Press, 1979) 47.
[6] Sandmel, 47.

Gentiles did not read Jewish writings, one cannot rule out the possibility that On the Life of Moses was addressed by Philo for the Gentile audience. It is not totally unlikely that Philo wrote with the hope that Gentiles would read his writings. He perhaps believed that when a biography of Moses, whose laws, after all, have "reached over the whole world," [7] were written in a way that Gentiles would acknowledge as being worthy of reading, then the Gentiles would read it. The theory that it was written for the Gentile audience is supported by Philo's introduction. Philo, when referring to the source material of his writing does not say "the elders of *our* nation" but rather "the elders of *my* nation."[8] From this, one is left to think that Philo did not merely limit himself to the Alexandrian Jews.

But whichever theory one may hold, Philo's influence was a lasting one. Thus, Paul Heinisch committed a book to describing one of the great influences of Philo; ie., on the church fathers. The book's title is Der Einfluss Philos auf die Älteste Christliche Exegese. In it he describes Philo with much praise: "Einer der einflußreichsten Männer seiner Zeit und einer der größten Gelehrten...."[9] Thus, with such interest-provoking introduction, Philo starts his description of the life of Moses.

In the Book I of On the Life of Moses, Philo depicts Moses primarily as a philosopher-king. And

---

[7]Philo, 192.
[8]Philo, 192. *Italics Mine*
[9]Paul Heinisch, Der Einfluss Philos Auf die Älteste Christliche Exegese (Münster: Verlag der Aschendorffschen Buchhandlung, 1908) 211.

since one would imagine the birth of a king to be special, Philo starts out with the birth of Moses. His parents are special as parents of a king should be. Thus, Philo writes, "And his father and mother were among the most excellent persons of their time...."[10] And Moses is an extraordinary child. He was so majestic that his parents wanted to keep him as long as possible despite the injunction by the Egyptian ruler that all Jewish male children must be killed. Philo describes, "...Moses, as soon as he was born, displayed a more beautiful and noble form than usual...."[11] Not only that, one of the reasons why the princess of Egypt decided to keep Moses as her child and also as an heir to her father's throne was the majestic quality of Moses, even as a child. Philo describes the reaction the princess had when she beheld Moses:

> And when the king's daughter saw that he was more perfect than could have been expected at his age, and when from his appearance she conceived greater good will than ever towards him, she adopted him as her son, having first put in practice all sorts of contrivances to increase the apparent bulk of her belly, so that he might be looked upon as her own genuine child, and not as a supposititious one....[12]

---

[10]Philo, 192.
[11]Philo, 193.
[12]Philo, 195.

Moses' majestic qualities extended further to his intellect as it should for a philosopher-king. He was taught arithmetic, geometry, music, and philosophy from Egyptians, "encyclical education" from the Greeks, and philosophies from Assyrian literature and astronomy from the Chaldaeans. And despite the fact that he had the means to do whatever he wanted in order to please himself, as in physical gratification, he involved himself in intellectual stimulation. [13] Philo spends much time in showing that Moses prepared himself to be the ideal ruler -- namely, the philosopher-king. Philo felt that only philosopher-kings could improve the conditions of their people. Thus, Philo agrees with others who espoused this view: "...some persons say, and not without some reason and propriety, that this is the only way by which cities can be expected to advance in improvement, if either the kings cultivate philosophy, or if philosophers exercise the kingly power." [14]

Furthermore, Philo, in harmony with his philosopher-king thesis, also did not neglect to show Moses preparing as a capable ruler. After Moses murdered the Egyptian who was particularly badgering and harming Jews and seeing that the king of Egypt was being tainted by bad advisors who misinformed on Moses, Moses left Egypt and went to the country of Arabia. There he was able to acquire leadership training by herding sheep. Philo explains,

> ...Moses took his father-in-law's herds and tended them, being thus instructed

---

[13] Philo, 196-197.
[14] Philo, 230.

in the lessons proper to qualify him for becoming the leader of a people, for the business of a shepherd is a preparation for the office of a king to any one who is destined to preside over that most manageable of all flocks, mankind, just as hunting is a good training school for men of warlike dispositions....[15]

Thus, Moses' preparation as the philospher-king was complete.

Moses put his preparation as a philosopher-king into practice when he led the Jews out of Egypt. One example of how Moses acted as a philosopher-king could be found in the passage about the Jews complaining to Moses when they perceived the Egyptian army pursuing them. The Jews did not have sufficient armor or weapons. And they were, in essence, trapped because the Egyptian army was pursuing them from the rear and there was Red Sea to the front of them. But Moses did not act harshly toward the Jews on account of their complaints; rather, he excused them. Furthermore, Moses communicated with God through his mind and placated his people with encouraging words.[16] So, as a true philosopher-king, Moses utilized his mind and employed reason rather than force. In this light, Philo places the king of Egypt in contrast to Moses. The king of Egypt was no philosopher-king. Rather than behaving with reason, he utilized force and

---

[15]Philo, 204-205.
[16]Philo, 217-218.

sought to induce people to fear. Philo describes: "The king...pursued after the Hebrews, thinking that he should subdue them by the mere shout of the battle."[17] This contrast makes the philosopher-king nature of Moses more evident.

Another factor that is closely tied with the concept of rule by reason for a philosopher-king is the idea that a philosopher-king has the consent of his people to legitimize his rule. He is, in essence, not a dictator who seizes power by force against the will of his people. Philo thus writes,

> Of all these men [Jews leaving Egypt], Moses was elected the leader; receiving the authority and sovereignty over them, not having gained it like some men who have forced their way to power and supremacy by force of arms and intrigue, and by armies of calvary and infantry, and by powerful fleets, but having been appointed for the sake of his virtue and excellence and that benevolence towards men which he was always feeling and exhibiting....[18]

Thus, Moses was a true philosopher-king.

Closely tied with the office of philosopher-king is the office of law giver. Philo shows Moses to be an ideal law giver, and this is demonstrated by the Mosaic Law. Philo thus writes,

---

[17]Philo, 217.
[18]Philo, 212.

> Now these four qualities are closely connected with and related to the legislative power, namely, humility, the love of justice, the love of virtue, and the hatred of iniquity; for every individual who has any desire for exercising his talents as a lawgiver is under the influence of each of these feelings. .... Therefore it is a very great thing if it has fallen to the lot of any one to arrive at any one of the qualities before mentioned, and it is a marvellous thing, as it should seem, for any one man to have been able to grasp them all, which in fact Moses appears to have been the only person who has ever done, having given a very clear description of the aforesaid virtues in the commandments which he established.[19]

And Moses is further praised by Philo for not losing that philosopher-king quality as the law giver. Moses appeals to reason rather than force. Accordingly, Philo writes: "For both in his commandments and also in his prohibitions he suggests and recommends rather than commands...desiring rather to allure men to virtue than to drive them to it...."[20] Because of such a superior law giver, the Mosaic Law is supreme; thus, not only the Jews but all other virtuous nations

---

[19]Philo, 231-232.
[20]Philo, 239.

"embrace" them. And this law exerts influence from one end of the spectrum to the other, "...all nations, barbarians, and Greeks...."[21] For example, Ptolemy Philadelphus -- who, according to Philo, was the "most excellent sovereign, not only of all those of his time, but of all that ever lived"[22] -- had the Mosaic Law translated into Greek. In essence, one can see the virtuousness of Moses as a recurring theme in On the Life of Moses. Thus, there is a constant reminder of the virtues of Moses. One is reminded of the stress Philo places on Moses exercising his mind and intellect rather than manipulating his circumstances to enjoy himself during his royal youth days in Egypt.

But being sceptical of the influence that Philo attributes to Moses as having exerted on sundry cultures, and particularly on that of the Greeks, Bréhier argues that Philo "borrowed" some ideas that existed at the time. Thus, according to Bréhier, influence is seen as going in the opposite direction. Bréhier writes,

> ...mais de fait, les traits par lesquels le dépeint Philon dans le deuxième livre de sa Vie, sont presque tous empruntés aux tradition populaire des Grecs, telles qu'elles se sont fixée chez Platon, chez les historiens et sourtout chez les neo-pythagoricien.[23]

---

[21]Philo, 233.
[22]Philo, 235.
[23]Bréhier, 18.

But one must keep in mind that although Philo might have borrowed some ideas from the Greeks, one cannot ignore the fact that Mosaic Law existed before the popular Greek culture and also that Mosaic Law had an influence on different cultures.

But Philo's great concentration on the traits of Moses led one another scholar to comment critically. Sandmel comments that Philo fashions the Scripture in a way to fit his thesis. Sandmel writes: "...Philo is quite discursive and very prone to explore the inner minds of his characters. Indeed it is no overstatement to suggest that his portrait of Moses uses the biblical account primarily as a point of departure for his own purposes."[24] One may say that he explores the minds of his characters and fashions the Scripture in a way to fit his thesis, but that view is a little bit harsh. For Philo is applying the holistic approach to the retelling of the life of Moses. It is more fair to say that Philo is applying his knowledge of the whole Scripture to the life story of Moses. For example, Moses is seen in the Scripture as having the Spirit that is worthy to be transfered to the seventy elders of Israel. This is seen in the episode concerning the quail. The people wanted to eat meat, so they complained. God told Moses that He would give meat to His people. And with this promise, God told Moses to bring seventy elders. And God "...took the Spirit that was on him [Moses] and put the Spirit on the seventy elders."[25] Not only that, the biblical concept of God as a holy being who requires holiness of His people[26] should

---

[24]Sandmel, 48.
[25]Numbers 11:25, The New International Version.
[26]Leviticus 11:44, The New International Version.

also be noted when studying Philo. When one puts these two factors together, one cannot think extreme the characteristics Philo attributes to Moses, who is said to have seen the holy God.

Moses, as noted before, is said to have seen God. This episode is found in Philo's description of Moses as the high priest. Thus, one can infer that Philo attributed great significance to this office of Moses. Accordingly, as a worthy chief priest should, Moses is seen as having practiced piety more than anybody else because he possessed natural qualities which enabled him to utilize philosophy to the utmost in the meditation and study of biblical doctrines. The result of such exertion by Moses was that he was able to practice virtue perfectly in words and actions. In turn, Moses "...was dear to God and devoted to God, being inspired by heavenly love, and honouring the Father of the universe above all things, and being in return honoured by him in a particular manner."[27]

Furthermore, Philo describes Moses as having purified himself both in mind and body before he was given that office. For forty days, Moses abstained from all meat and drink and relations with women. And as he contemplated the commands of God, Moses was purified first in his mind and then in his body, so that when he came down from Mount Sinai forty days afterwards, people who saw him were amazed, and they could not endure to look at him. And it was on the mountain that Moses "...was initiated in the sacred will of God, being instructed in

---

[27] Philo, 244.

all the most important matters which relate to his priesthood..."[28]

There is, however, some scholarly disagreement concerning the Sinai episode and the induction of Moses into priesthood. Sandmel focuses on the human efforts of Moses. Accordingly, Sandmel writes: "The Sinai episode for Philo is essentially an unique example of the achievement of Moses through his reason, rather than only a supernatural intervention and revelation of laws on the part of the Deity."[29] But, Heinisch disagrees, attributing the origin of all the special qualities of Moses to God. Therefore, he writes, "Alle weltliche und geistliche Macht war ihm [Moses] von Gott übertragen...."[30] In light of Philo's writings, one is left to believe that Heinisch is more in keeping with the thoughts of Philo. For even when Philo writes about Moses dedicating himself to God, Philo does not attribute that ability innately to Moses or his reason, but rather to a supernatural force. Thus, Philo writes, "Therefore, he [Moses]...was dear to God and devoted to God, *being inspired by heavenly love*...."[31] Furthermore, Philo writes that Moses was given the honor "...to *be allowed* to serve the true and living God."[32] There is more. Philo writes that Moses was "*initiated* in the sacred will of God."[33] In all of these cases, Moses is

---

[28]Philo, 245.
[29]Sandmel, 50.
[30]Heinisch, 211.
[31]Philo, 244. *Italics Mine.*
[32]Philo, 244-245. *Italics Mine.*
[33]Philo, 245. *Italics Mine.*

the subject of a passive verb that implies the main actor or motivator to be God.

And on Mount Sinai, Moses was given instructions about how to construct a temple and furnish it. Here, one can see the allegorist in Philo come alive. One such example is with the two cherubim. Philo says that one represents the creative power of God, called God, and the other represents the kingly power of God, called Lord.[34] Also, Philo explains that the dress of a high priest is representative of the world; thus, he says, "Such, then, is the dress of the high priest. .... In its whole it is a copy and representation of the world; and the parts are a representation of the separate parts of the world."[35] In his descriptions of the dress for the high priest, Philo attributes a great significance to numbers. They are symbolic of something greater. For example, Philo elaborately explains the significance of the twelve stones on the breast of the robe of the high priest:

> Then the twelve stones on the breast, which are not like one another in colour, and which are divided into four rows of three stones in each, what else can they be emblems of, except of the circle of the zodiac? For that also is divided into four parts, each consisting of three animals, by which divisions it makes up the seasons of the year, spring, summer, autumn, and

---

[34]Philo, 251.
[35]Philo, 254.

> winter, distinguishing the four changes, the two solstices, and the two equinoxes, each of which has its limit of three signs of this zodiac, by the revolutions of the sun, according to that unchangeable, and most lasting, and really divine ratio which exists in numbers; on which account they attached it to that which is with great propriety called the logeum.[36]

Thus, one could see that Philo was greatly interested in the underlying significance of visible objects.

In the beginning of the second book of <u>On the Life of Moses</u>, Philo had ascribed the office of prophecy as one of the four offices ascribed to Moses; but Philo does not really dedicate a large section for expounding this office, whereas he does so for the office of philosopher-king, law giver, and priest. The reason is that the office of prophecy is closely tied to that of priesthood. Harry Austryn Wolfson believes that Philo had become acquainted with the scriptural concept of prophecy before Philo had been exposed to popular writings of his day -- like Homer, Plato, and the Stoics. Philo's ultimate belief had, as the foundation, the Scripture, but that foundation was reshaped and expressed in the philosophical concepts of his day. According to Wolfson, prophecy as perceived by Philo is, first, the power to predict the future, as Moses' prediction of the successful crossing of the Red Sea. Second, prophecy is the power of knowing what rites and prayers are to be done to

---

[36]Philo, 255.

appease God and avert God's punishment. Third, prophecy is "...the power to receive from God certain communications by which men were to be guided in their life."[37] Wolfson claims that Moses was a prophet in the sense of priest because Moses, as a priest, knew sacred rites and divine service by which he could avert evil from the Jews. This certainly corresponds to the propitiatory function of prophets. Moses, as a prophet-priest, also had a direct vision as to how the sanctuary should appear and how it should be furnished. So like a prophet, Moses received direct "communication" from God for the guidance of the Jewish people.[38] Thus, one can see that the office of prophet is intermingled with the office of priest.

    In essence, however, these four offices of Moses are combined and intertwined. Heinisch comments: "...alle Ämter, zu denen Gott jemals seine Auserwählten berufen hat, wurden von ihm verwaltet, und während sonst eine Teilung der Ämter stattfindet, so daß dem einen dieses, dem andern jenes anvertraut wird, vereinigte Moses alle in seiner Person." [39] Sundry offices of Moses legitimize each other. Bréhier shows that the office of the law giver is legitimized by other offices of Moses: "Chez Philon, Moïse n'est législateur que parce qu'il est d'abord roi. C'est comme roi qu'il prend toutes les fonctions humaines et divines, puisqu'il est comme tel,

---

[37] Harry Austryn Wolfson, Philo: Foundations of Religious Philosophy in Judaism, Christianity, and Islam (Volume 2) (Cambridge, Massachusetts: Harvard University Press, 1947) 11-12.
[38] Wolfson, (Volume 2), 19-20.
[39] Heinisch, 211.

législateur et grand prêtre."[40] That is why the theme of Moses' virtues runs throughout On the Life of Moses. From youth, the time in which Moses was more active in fostering the intellectual, philosophical aspect of self rather than indulging in the pleasures of the senses, to the conferral of the priesthood, the office which required the virtues, which philosophy-cultivated field of "natural qualities"[41] brings to perfection, the theme of purity of mind and body is ever present.

From Philo's description of Moses, one may perceive Moses as supra-human, and even as divine. Ronald Williamson feels that Philo would attribute θεο'ς to Moses "...because of the close association in Philo's mind, amounting at times to an identification, of Moses and the logos."[42] And even in Philo's writing, one can see that Moses is referred to as a god. Philo writes, "For he [Moses] also was called the god and king of the whole nation...."[43] Bréhier feels that Philo was influenced by his surroundings in granting Moses divine attribute; thus, he comments,

> ...Philon, probablement sous l'influence d'autres idées contemporaines, tendait à réaliser dans l'empereur la figure du roi idéal; nous allons bientôt en rencontrer d'autres. Le pouvoir

---

[40]Bréhier, 19.
[41]Philo, 244.
[42]Ronald Williamson, Jews in the Hellenistic World: Philo (Cambridge, Great Britain: Cambridge University Press, 1989) 55.
[43]Philo, 215.

> royal est de nature divine; Moïse est l'élu de Dieu...pourtant avec l'acceptation de la volonté populaire, qui vient elle-même en ce cas de l'inspiration divine. C'est dans la monarchie divine que le roi doit prendre son modèle. Il est le dieu de qu'il ses sujets. Philon admet ici pour son compte le raisonnement qu'il prête à Caligula, lorsque ce mauvais empereur s'assimile aux dieux....[44]

Although one could make the claim that Philo was attributing divine qualities to Moses, one cannot say that he believed in the concept of incarnation. Philo did not believe that God became man in Moses. Since flesh and spirit were two opposed qualities, Philo's concept of deification of Moses was one in which the flesh part of Moses would gradually and completely be eradicated from the life of Moses.[45] This concept of Philo can be found in the death of Moses. Philo writes: "...when he [Moses] was about to depart from hence to heaven...the Father...changed him, having previously been a double being, composed of soul and body, into the nature of a single body, transforming him wholly and entirely into a most sun-like mind...."[46]

Thus, besides the four offices held by Moses, Philo adds the divine characteristic to Moses. Such was the admiration and respect that Philo ascribed to

---

[44]Bréhier, 21.
[45]Williamson, 117-118.
[46]Philo, 269.

Moses. From the birth of Moses to the death of Moses, Philo portrayed him as an ideal being. Burton L. Mack aptly summarizes the significance of Moses for Philo: "Moses is in fact such an important figure for Philo that he becomes the prime manifestation not only of the logos, but of the *sophos*, the *theios aner*, the cultural hero, the ideal being, the chief priest, hierophant, and prophet of God."[47]

---

[47]Burton L. Mack, "Imitatio Mosis," Studia Philonica (Volume 1) (Chicago: The Philo Institute, Inc., 1972, pp. 27-55) 33. *Italics Not Mine.*

Bibliography

Bréhier, Émile. Les Idées Philosophique et Religieuses de Philon d'Alexandrie. Paris: Librairie Philosophique J. Vrin, 1950.

Harrington, Daniel J. Pseudo-Philon: Les Antiquités Bibliques (Tome 1). Paris: Les Éditions du Cerf, 1976.

Hay, David M. "Philo's Reference to Other Allegorists." Studia Philonica (Volume 6). Chicago: The Philo Institute, Inc., 1980, pp. 41-75.

Heinisch, Paul. Der Einfluss Philos Auf die Älteste Christliche Exegese. Münster: Verlag der Aschendorffschen Buchhandlung, 1908.

Mack, Burton L. "Imitatio Mosis." Studia Philonica (Volume 1). Chicago: The Philo Institute, Inc., 1972, pp. 27-55.

Otte, Klaus. Das Sprachverständnis bei Philo von Alexandrien. Tübingen: J. C. B. Mohr (Paul Siebeck), 1968.

Philo Judaeus. "On the Life of Moses." The Essential Philo. Ed. Nahum N. Glatzer. New York: Schocken Books, 1971, pp. 190-270.

Sandmel, Samuel. Philo of Alexandria: An Introduction. New York: Oxford University Press, 1979.

Williamson, Ronald. Jews in the Hellenistic World: Philo. Cambridge, Great Britain: Cambridge University Press, 1989.

Wolfson, Harry Austryn. Philo: Foundations of Religious Philosophy in Judaism, Christianity, and Islam (Volume 1). Cambridge, Massachusetts: Harvard University Press, 1947.

Wolfson, Harry Austryn. Philo: Foundations of Religious Philosophy in Judaism, Christianity and Islam (Volume 2) Cambridge, Massachusetts: Harvard University Press, 1947.

--------- The Holy Bible (The New International Version). New York: New York International Bible Society, 1978.

"A Paradigmatic Shift in the Redemptive Medium of the Law: Paul's Thoughts as a Bridge"[1]

The Law has been a central redemptive medium from the times of the ancient Hebrews to the Judaisms of the first century AD. But one "Jewish" movement, which came to be called Christianity, came to view the Law in a different light from other Judaisms; for Christians, there was a paradigmatic shift in the redemptive medium of the Law.

In fact, Jesus, the founder of the sect, did claim his interpretation of the Law as authoritative, but he did not deny the goodness of the Law. Paul, on the other hand, seemed to reassess the value of the Law. Such phenomena prompted scholars to comment on the nature of the Law within the early Christian community. I will discuss the "covenantal nomism" concept of E. P. Sanders, the idea of faith being the criterion for "getting in" and "staying in" by James Dunn, and the freedom-obligation thesis by C. K. Barrett. Upon examination of these scholars, I will propose that their explanation of the Law is inadequate for explaining the paradigmatic shift.

---

[1] This paper was presented at the New Testament section of the 1996 Pacific Coast meeting of the Society of Biblical Literature meeting held at the University of California, San Diego (UCSD). I would like to thank the chair of the section, Professor Ronald Hock of the University of Southern California, for his helpful comments and positive encouragement.

How did Christ come to replace the Law as the redemptive medium for a community that held to the Old Testament as their scripture? By the mid-second century AD, Christian thinkers justified their actions by identifying Christ with the Law. This was an innovation because never before did anyone hypostastically represent in a historical person the embodiment of a concept that provided redemptive value on the same social level as did a general concept, such as the Law.

There are precedents for hypostastic representation of concepts within Judaism, the Graeco-Roman culture, and in the Gospel of John. But, the hypostastic representations provided in these examples in no way functioned in the same social extent that Christ as the Law did by mid-second century.

When one examines Paul's thoughts, however, it becomes clear how Christians came to hypostastically represent Jesus Christ as the Law with all the power and social significance attached to the Law. Although Paul does not call Jesus Christ the Law, he lays the foundation by attaching social and redemptive significance to Jesus Christ that the Law possessed in the Jewish tradition. This becomes clear when one examines Paul's concept of baptism, the Lord's Supper, and his general theology of unity in Christ, with close attention to Galatians 3:26-29.

Throughout the history of Israelites, the Mosaic Law functioned to provide identity and a point of reference. In other words, the Mosaic Law proved to be a redemptive medium for the Israelites. Although different interpretations provided time for discussion, no Jew questioned the innate value and authority of the Law. The Law of God was holy and pure.

But with early Christianity, a controversy concerning the Law arose. It started with Jesus of Nazareth, who claimed an authority greater than that of Moses in "The Sermon on the Mount." Jesus boldly stated: "You have heard that it was said.... But I tell you...."[2] Despite his audacious claim to interpret the Law, Jesus did not undermine the fundamental value of the law. Jesus reassures the reader before his interpretation:

> Do not think that I have come to abolish the Law or the Prophets; I have not come to abolish them but to fulfill them. I tell you the truth, until heaven and earth disappear, not the smallest letter, not the smallest stroke of a pen, will by any means disappear from the Law until everything is accomplished. Anyone who breaks one of the least of these commandments and teaches others to do the same will

---

[2] Matthew 5:21f, 27f, 33f, 38f,43f (NIV). There is another passage that basically has the same concept but is phrased differently: "It has been said.... But I tell you..." (Matthew 5:31f NIV). This belongs to *Sitz im Leben*, level 1 (that is, to Jesus). First of all, no Jewish person tried to assert greater authority than that of Moses. Secondly, early Christian writers utilized the Hebrew Scriptures in support of their arguments in contrast to Jesus' asserting authority over that of Moses, the most important figure in the Hebrew Scriptures, who has first five books of the Hebrew Scriptures attributed to him.

be called least in the kingdom of heaven, but whoever practices and teaches these commands will be called great in the kingdom of heaven.[3]

Thus, one could argue that Jesus was actually offering different interpretation of the Law rather than going against the fundamental authority or value of the Law.

But with Paul's writing, one sees radically differing perception of the Law. Paul attacks the value of the law: "But now, by dying to what once bound us, we have been released from the law so that we serve in the new way of the Spirit, and not in the old ways of the written code."[4] Paul, thus, depicts Law as something that is old and no longer applicable. But soon afterwards, Paul offers conflicting sentiments towards the law: "What shall we say, then? Is the law sin? Certainly not!"[5] Paul further defends

---

[3]Matthew 5:17-19 (NIV). This belongs to *Sitz im Leben*, level one, under the historical scrutiny of the criterion of double dissimilarity. First of all, Jesus' claim that he came to fulfill the Law and not abolish it goes against the grain of Judaism of his time. Jews of the time did not perceive the law as something that could be destroyed because they believed that the Law, given by God, was eternal and must be kept. Secondly, the determination of one's place in the kingdom of heaven on the basis of one's observation of the Law goes against the early Christian teachings. If this were the case, Peter and Paul who actively associated with and shared table fellowship with Gentiles would be liable, as would those among the twelve who did not observe the Sabbath Day in the way prescribed by Jewish laws.
[4]Romans 7:6 (NIV).
[5]Romans 7:7 (NIV).

the law: "So then, the law is holy, and the commandment is holy, righteous and good."[6] Not only does Paul defend the Law, he denigrates himself in the process of showing the Law to be good:

> Did that which is good, then, become death to me? By no means! .... We know that the law is spiritual; but I am unspiritual, sold as a slave to sin. I do not understand what I do. For what I want to do I do not do, but what I hate I do.[7]

One can see, therefore, that although Paul does seem to deny the continuing value of the law, he struggles with himself to figure out the exact nature of the Law, which was, after all, given by God and, therefore, good.

Scholars throughout the long history of Christianity attempted to offer viable explanation of Paul's perception of the Law within the nascent Christian movement. What function does the Law have on becoming a member of the Christian community? What function does the Law have once a person is a member of the Christian community? In this paper, I will discuss three differing positions; namely, those held by E. P. Sanders, James D. Dunn, and C. K. Barrett.

E. P. Sanders, with the phrase, "covenantal nomism," attempts to explain the relationship of the Law to the early Christian community. To put it

---

[6]Romans 7:12 (NIV).
[7]Romans 7:13a, 14-15 (NIV).

simply, Sanders feels that "getting in" to a Christian community did not require keeping the Law, but "staying in" did. Sanders writes:

> The diagram will, I hope, make it clear that Paul used the term *nomos* in at least two quite distinct contexts, one in discussing how one gets 'in' (not by works of law), the other in discussing how one who is 'in' behaves (he keeps the law).[8]

Sanders, however, states that Paul was not specifically arguing in favor of faith nor of the Law. For Sanders, Galatians 3 serves as proof:

> The argument of Galatians 3 is against Christian missionaries, not against Judaism, and it is against the view that Gentiles must accept the law *as a condition* of or as a basic requirement for membership Paul's argument is not in favor of faith per se, nor is it against requiring the Gentiles to keep the law of Moses in order to be true "sons of Abraham."[9]

Rather, Sanders emphasizes that "*Gentiles are righteoused by faith*" in Paul's thought and that Paul's proof text is found in Galatians 3 with the example of

---

[8] E. P. Sanders, Paul, the Law, and the Jewish People (Philadelphia: Fortress Press, 1983) 10.
[9] Sanders 19 (Italics Not Mine).

the Abraham story.[10] To further support his claims, Sanders claims that even the Jews were "righteoused by faith" in the thoughts of Paul. In fact, God's eternal plan is constant in that righteousness is not determined by the Law:

> That Paul's viewpoint is that of God's eternal plan of salvation is seen even more clearly in Gal. 3.15-26, where the law and faith are assigned their places in the history of salvation. .... Thus the whole thrust of the argument is that righteousness was never, in God's plan, intended to be by the law.[11]

Thus, for Sanders, faith served as means of getting into the Christian community, but the Law served as a standard for living once someone was in.

James D. Dunn does not agree with Sanders' perception of the Law. Dunn believes that, for Paul, the Law is neither the requirement for inclusion in the community nor for staying in that community. Dunn writes:

> The significance of Paul's stand should not be underestimated. For the first time probably, he had come to see that the principle of "justification through faith" applied not simply to the acceptance of the gospel in conversion, but

---

[10]Sanders 21 (Italics for the Quote Not Mine).
[11]Sanders 26-27.

also to the whole of the believer's life. That is to say, he saw that justification through faith was not simply a statement of how the believer entered into God's covenanted promises (the understanding of the gospel agreed at Jerusalem); it must also regulate his life as a believer.[12]

Dunn holds strongly to his idea that Paul viewed faith as the criterion for "getting in" and "staying in." Thus, Dunn criticizes Sanders' view of covenantal nomism. Dunn believes that the idea that faith is the requirement for "getting in," but the Law was the requirement for "staying in" is inconsistent:

> The covenantal nomism of Judaism and of the Jewish believers (life in accordance with the law within the covenant given by grace...) was in fact a contradiction of that agreed understanding of justification through faith. To live life "in Christ" *and* "in accordance with the law" was not possible; it involved a basic contradiction in terms and in the understanding of what made someone acceptable to God. Thus, Paul began to see, as probably he had never seen before, that the principle of justification through faith meant a redefining of the relation between the

---

[12]James D. G. Dunn, Jesus, Paul and the Law (Louisville, Kentucky: Westminster/John Knox Press, 1990) 158-9.

> believer and Israel -- *not* an abandoning of that link.... To begin with the Spirit and through faith rules out not just justification by works of law, but life lived by law (covenantal nomism) also -- the very argument which he develops in the rest of Galatians.[13]

Thus, Dunn emphasizes faith as the only point of reference for Christians. Dunn uses Galatians 2:16 in support of his idea that Paul rejected the concept of covenantal nomism. This is brought out clearly in the Galatians 2:16 passage that Dunn provides in his book:

> "...knowing that a man is not justified from works of the law *except* through faith in Jesus Christ, we have believed in Christ Jesus in order that we might be justified from faith in Christ, and *not* from works of law..."[14]

The first part of the quote shows the Law and faith working harmoniously, but Dunn pushes this aside with the second part of the translation, which places the Law and faith in opposition. Thus, one can see that Dunn spends much careful detail to distinguish himself from Sanders' perception of the Law.

    C. K. Barrett uses a different approach in his discussion of the Law. Whereas Sanders and Dunn discuss the relationship between the requirement of

---

[13]Dunn 159 (Italics Not Mine).
[14]Dunn 196 (Italics Not Mine).

the Law and the Christian community, Barrett ponders the concept of freedom from the Law in the context of the Christian community. Barrett believes that freedom for a Christian is necessarily accomplished by obligation. Barrett writes:

> It is all the more important to attend to the relation between the two: freedom, and obligation. Freedom is a concept that calls for wholeness. I am not a fully free member of society if I am restricted whether politically or economically, and I am not a fully free person if I am not a member of a fully free society, if that is, I exercise my freedom at the expense of others. This means that freedom, true freedom, is always and necessarily accompanied by obligation, a term as unpopular as freedom is popular -- that is, when it is applied to myself.[15]

---

[15] C. K. Barrett, Freedom and Obligation: A Study of the Epistle to the Galatians (London: SPCK, 1985) 1. Compare with the concept of Libertas in the traditional Roman sense. Look at Gerd Tellenbach's Church, State and Christian Society at the time of the Investiture Contest, trans. R. F. Bennett (Toronto: University of Toronto Press, 1991). Tellenbach writes: "Cicero, in the De Re Publica, showed clearly what he understood by a free people.... The Romans dated their their freedom from the expulsion of the kings and the assumption of authority by the people. Legal differences of status gradually disappeared, so that classical Roman freedom meant the equal participation of all citizens in self-government. Freedom consisted in each man surrendering to others as much power over himself as others for their part surrendered to him, and this found practical expression

Barrett assumes that a Christian is free from the Law. But this freedom entails obligation to other members of the Christian community.

But the greatest distinction that Barrett possesses from Sanders and Dunn is his willingness to acknowledge that Paul believed that justification by the Law was, in fact, possible. Barrett writes:

> Paul is prepared to allow -- he does so explicitly in Romans 2 -- that justifycation by law is theoretically possible. He seems not yet (in Galatians) to have seen the further point that he goes on to make in Romans, that it is possible to look back at the law from the vantage point of the Christian's knowledge of Christ and see that the law does bear witness to him and, rightly understood, seeks the same response as the Gospel, namely faith.[16]

Thus, one can see that Barrett perceives the Law and faith in harmonious relationship. Paul believes that justification by the Law is possible because it is intended to produce faith, but in Galatians, he does not argue that far. Barrett, therefore, stands in contrast to Sanders and Dunn, both of whom agree that inclusion or the initial membership requirement is

---

when each citizen had his turn in office and his share in legislative action. All were free, for none was bound more than another by the self-imposed law" (11).
[16]Barrett 62-63.

faith and not the Law. Sanders and Dunn place the Law in contrast to faith, whereas Barrett describes them working harmoniously.

Despite the differences, all the scholars discussed above have one thing in common; their focus is on the Law. They are concerned with the requirement of the Law, or the lack thereof, in conjunction with the Christian community. They quietly brush aside how the Law, which functioned as redemptive medium for the Israelites for many, many years, ceased to hold such great value in a period of less than a hundred years. First of all, Sanders uses *a priori* argumentation from Galatians to show that God always functioned in a relationship that could be described with the phrase "covenantal nomism" -- entrance never required the Law but living as a member of the covenant community did. Dunn throws out the Law as a whole, leaving the reader to wonder, "Could such radical shift be possible with Paul, considering his background and also his other writings?" Barrett plays around with ideas of freedom and obligation to show how Christian community functions in an important way to provide a point of reference for Christians. One can see that Barrett is taking the easy road out by ignoring the Law and stating that the Law produces faith. Sanders, Dunn, and Barrett do not have any definitive explanation describing the early Christian perception of the Law and also the process by which such radical shift took place from the perception in the Old Testament.

The problem of the significance of the Law as redemptive medium becomes more poignant in light of literature from early Christian fathers. Early Christian fathers hypostastically identified Jesus Christ as the Law. Thereby, they maintained the value of the Law as a redemptive medium. But since they equated the Law hypostastically with Christ, the chief redemptive medium was, in fact, Christ. Clement of Alexandria's writings show this: "'Quoting the Preaching of Peter you will find the Lord called Law and Word (νομος και λογος)' (*Strom.* I, 182:3)"[17] *Eclogae Propheticae* also contains a reference that shows the Law hypostastically as Jesus Christ. Old Testament is also utilized in support of this representation:

> a passage from the *Eclogae Propheticae* adds an interesting point: "The Lord is himself called Law and Word according to Peter in the *Kerygma*, and also according to the Prophet who writes: the Law (νομος) shall go out from Sion and the Word of God from Jerusalem (*Is.* 2: 3)" (*Ecl. Proph.* 58). The mention of the text from Isaiah is the more interesting, since it occurs also in the primitive *testimonia*.[18]

Justin also interprets Isaiah 2:3 as prophetic of Christ. Justin perceives the Law described in Isaiah as hypostastically representing Jesus Christ:

---

[17] Jean Daniélou, The Theology of Jewish Christianity, trans. John A. Baker (London: Darton, Longman & Todd, 1964) 164.
[18] Daniélou 164.

In Justin the Lord is called νομος with reference to the same text. Thus in the *Dial.* XXIV, I he writes "There is now another covenant; another Law has gone forth from Sion, Jesus Christ." Justin again refers to Isaiah, though not to the same passage, a little further on: "The Son of God ... Christ ... was proclaimed as about to come as an everlasting Law (νομος) and new Covenant for the whole world" (*Dial.* XLIII, I).[19]

Daniélou assures that referring to Jesus Christ as the Law and Covenant is deeply ingrained in Justin's thoughts. Daniélou writes:

It will be noticed that Christ is here called at the same time both Law and Covenant (διαθηκη). This conjuncttion had already been made in *Dial.* XI, 2: "As an external and final (τελευταιος) Law was Christ given, and this Covenant is sure, after which there is no law, or ordinance, or command.[20]

Daniélou believes that such hypostastic identification of the Law with Christ was an innovation; for, the New Testament only goes on so far as to say that

---

[19] Daniélou 164-5.
[20] 165.

Christ introduced the definitive Law. Daniélou writes:

> The concept of Christ as introducing a new covenant and bringing in the definitive Law was current in the New Testament. But the interest of the texts quoted here lies in the fact that they add a new element, the personal identification of the Son of God with the Law and the Covenant.[21]

Indeed, equating the Law with Jesus was an innovation. But are there any precedents where an abstract concept, such as the Law, is represented hypostastically?

One can gather from Judaism, Roman and Greek culture, and Christianity some examples where a concept is given hypostastic quality. In Judaism, one can find examples of hypostastic representation of concepts. For example, in Proverbs, the writer represents wisdom in a hypostastic way. It is written in Proverbs: "Wisdom calls aloud in the street, she raises her voice in the public squares, at the head of noisy streets she cries out, in the gateways of the city she makes her speech...."[22] In chapter eight of Proverbs, one can see similar phenomena of hypostastic representation of a concept: "Does not wisdom call out? Does not understanding raise her voice?"[23] It is clear that there are precedents in the

---

[21] 165.
[22] Proverbs 1:20f (NIV).
[23] Proverbs 8:1 (NIV).

Jewish culture for hypostastic representation of a concept.

There is a better example found in Philo. Philo depicts Moses as a hypostastic embodiment of holiness and goodness; thus, he refers to Moses as a god. Philo writes: "For he [Moses] also was called the god and king of the whole nation...."[24] Ronald Williamson feels that Philo describes Moses as θεος "...because of the close association in Philo's mind, amounting at times to an identification, of Moses and the logos."[25] One can further see this in Philo's description of transformation of Moses just before Moses' death. Philo describes Moses as losing his physical attributes; Moses was left only with spiritual qualities embodied in the logos. Philo writes:

> when he [Moses] was about to depart from hence to heaven...the Father...changed him, having previously been a double being, composed of soul and body, into the nature of a single body, transforming him wholly and entirely into a most sun-like mind.[26]

It is clear that Philo is interested not merely in symbolically representing Philo as a hypostastic embodiment of the logos, but depicting this embodi-

---

[24]Philo Judaeus, "On the Life of Moses," The Essential Philo, ed. Nahum N. Glatzer (New York: Schocken Books, 1971, pp. 190-270) 215.
[25]Jews in the Hellenistic World: Philo (Cambridge, Great Britain: Cambridge University Press, 1989) 55.
[26]Philo 269.

ment as a real occurrence as the result of divine intervention.

Émil Bréhier feels that Philo was influenced by his surroundings in granting Moses divine attributes; thus, he comments:

> Philon, probablement sous l'influence d'autres idées contemporaines, tendait à réaliser dans l'empereur la figure du roi idéal; nous allons bientôt en rencontrer d'autres. Le pouvoir royal est de nature divine; Moïse est l'élu de Deu...pourtant avec l'acceptance de la volonté populaire, qui vient elle-même en ce cas de l'inspiration divine. C'est dans la monarchie divine que le roi doit prendre son modèle. Il est le dieu de qu'il ses sujets. Philon admet ici pour son compte le raisonnement qu'il prête à Caligula, lorsque ce mauvais empereur s'assimile aux dieux....[27]

No doubt, living in an eclectic society, Philo was well aware of ideas and customs of his times, but one must not be quick to rule out the influence of Jewish traditions in impacting his thoughts. For example, it was mentioned previously that the book of Proverbs hypostastically represented wisdom. Philo was aware of this wisdom tradition.

In fact, for Philo, Moses was a hypostastic embodiment of and representation of all that was

---

[27] Les idées philosophique et religieuse de Philon d"Alexandrie (Paris: Librairie Philosophique J. Vrin, 1950) 21.

good -- an ideal being. Burton Mack summarizes the significance of Moses for Philo:

> Moses is in fact such an important figure for Philo that he becomes the prime manifestation not only of the logos, but of the *sophos*, the *theios aner*, the cultural hero, the ideal being, the chief priest, hierophant, and prophet of God.[28]

One can see that hypostastic representation of a concept, such as logos and wisdom, was very much a part of the Jewish culture.

The Graeco-Roman culture also had examples of hypostastic representation of concepts. One example can be found in Hesiod's *Works and Days*, written around 700 BC. Hesiod represents the concept of justice as a goddess. Hesiod writes:

> But you, Perses, listen to right and do not foster violence; for violence is bad for a common man. Even a noble cannot easily bear its burden, but is weighed down under it when he has fallen into delusion. The better path is to go by on the other side towards justice; for [Dike, Goddess of] Justice beats Outrage when she comes at length to the end of the race. But only when he has suffered does the fool

---

[28]"Imitatio Mosis," Studia Philonica (Volume 1) (Chicago: The Philo Institute, Inc., 1972, pp. 27-55) 33. Italics Not Mine.

> learn this. For Oath keeps pace with wrong judgments. There is a noise when Justice is being dragged in the way where those who devour bribes and give sentence with crooked judgments take her. And she, wrapped in mist, follows to the city and haunts of the people, weeping, and bringing mischief to men, even to such as have driven her forth in that they did not deal straightly with her.[29]

One can see that justice took on a hypostastic quality in the same way wisdom did in the book of Proverbs. In the Greek tradition, however, Justice is represented in a hypostastic way as a goddess, whereas in the book of Proverbs, wisdom only takes on a female hypostasis.

The Roman world also provides examples of hypostastic representation of concepts. One such example is found in Octavian's name, Augustus, which was conferred on him by the senate. The new name represented hypostastic embodiment in the person of Octavian of all the qualities belonging to the word *augustus*. Dio Cassius describes:

> The name Augustus was at length bestowed upon him by the senate and by the people. ...[he] took the title of "Augustus," signifying that he was

---

[29]Nels M. Bailkey (ed.), <u>Readings in Ancient History: Thought and Experience from Gilgamesh to St. Augustine</u> (Lexington, Massachusetts: D. C. Health and Company, 1992) 142.

> more than human; for all the most precious and sacred objects are termed *augusta*. Therefore they addressed him also in Greek as *Sebastos*, meaning an *august* personage, from the passive of the verb *sebazo*, "to revere."[30]

Thus, one can see that the Graeco-Roman world provided examples of hypostastic representation of concepts.

The New Testament also has an example of hypostastic representation of a concept in the gospel of John. The writer of the gospel depicts the logos, or the word, in a hypostastic way:

> In the beginning was the Word, and the Word was with God, and the Word was God. .... The Word became flesh and lived for a while among us. We have seen his glory, the glory of the one and only Son, who came from the Father, full of grace and truth. John testifies concerning him. He cries out, saying, "This was he of whom I said, 'He who comes after me has surpassed me because he was before

---

[30]Ronald Mellor (ed.), From Augustus to Nero: The First Dynasty of Imperial Rome (East Lansing, Michigan: Michigan State University Press, 1990) 41.

me.'" ...grace and truth came through Jesus Christ.[31]

This hypostastic representation of the logos as Jesus Christ is different from other examples in that the gospel writer claims the taking on of flesh by the logos; in other words, incarnation. This stands in contrast to thoughts of the times. Philo shows Moses to be a hypostastic representation of the logos, but he does so by diminishing the value of the flesh. This is in keeping with Stoicism, a prevalent thinking of the times, which painted material world in a negative light and glorified the spiritual world of the divine reason. Furthermore, other examples, such as wisdom and the name "Augustus," toyed with symbolism rather than a physical incorporation. Even the goddess Justice, although described with human attributes, would never be seen as "justice becoming flesh." But despite differences among the examples, one fact remains; that is, one can find examples of hypostastic representation of concepts in the Jewish, the Graeco-Roman, and the New Testament world.

---

[31] John 1:1, 14-15, 17b (NIV). Notice that the contents of verse 15 is reiterated in verse 30, which is contained in a passage dealing with John the Baptizer's encounter with Jesus of Nazareth. In verse 30, the writer of the gospel places on the lips of John the Baptizer: "This is the one I meant when I said, 'A man who comes after me has surpassed me because he was before me." This is significant in that the writer emphasizes the hypostastic representation of the logos in the person of Jesus of Nazareth. Although Jesus was conceived six months later than John the Baptizer, Jesus Christ, as the eternal logos in the eyes of the gospel writer of John, preceded John the Baptizer.

But what is the connection between these examples and the hypostastic representation of Jesus Christ as the Law? This question becomes harder to answer in light of the fact that the Law held a redemptive significance for the Jews. Not only did the Law outline proper religious and social behavior, it functioned as a source of identity. None of the examples provided from Jewish, Graeco-Roman, and New Testament traditions functions as redemptive media -- a source a identity providing a redeeming value. One that comes closest to it may be the logos if one views the concept through the Stoic lense, because the Stoics considered the logos, or the divine reason, as a source of pantheistic identification for all those who could reason. But Stoicism does not hypostastically represent the logos. Furthermore, the gospel of John shows hypostastic representation in the incarnation of the logos into one person, Jesus Christ. This begs the question, "How could the logos represented hypostastically in Jesus Christ function as a redemptive medium in the similar sociological way for Christians as the Law did for the Jews?"

Are there any examples from the early Christian tradition that would help one to understand the dynamics of the hypostastic representation of the Law as Jesus Christ in later stages of historical development? When one concentrates on the former function of the Law -- a source of redeeming identification for the Israelites -- one can see a resemblance with the early Christian traditions, especially in the thoughts of Paul. Paul emphasizes a redeeming identification with the person of Jesus Christ. And this, in turn, shows how Paul functions as a bridge between the perception of the Law by the Jews and the perception of Christ as the Law by the Christians. Paul expounds on the significance of baptism, the Lord's Supper, and his general theological rumination to show the significance of Jesus Christ as a redemptive medium.

Paul uses baptism to show that Jesus Christ functions as a source of redemptive identification. Paul writes:

> Don't you know that all of us who were baptized into Christ Jesus were baptized into his death? We were therefore buried with him through baptism into death in order that, just as Christ was raised from the dead through the glory of the Father, we too may live a new life. If we have been united with him in his death, we will certainly be united with him in his resurrection. .... The death he [Jesus Christ] died, he died to sin once for all; but the life he lives, he lives to God. In the same way, count yourselves dead to sin but alive to God in Christ Jesus.[32]

Thus, baptism symbolizes one's participating in Christ -- more specifically, in his death and resurrection. But Jesus' death, as well as believers' symbolic death in him, represents death to sin, and

---

[32]Romans 6:3-5, 10-11 (NIV).

Jesus' resurrected life, as well as believers' life, represents life lived for God.

For Paul, baptism of believers represents communal identification in Jesus Christ. Paul uses the imagery of the body to accomplish this:

> The body is a unit, though it is made up of many parts; and though all its parts are many, they form one body. So it is with Christ. For we were all baptized by one Spirit into one body -- whether Jews or Greeks, slave or free -- and we were all given the one Spirit to drink.[33]

Thus, one can see that, symbolically, all believers are incorporated into Christ in Paul's thoughts.

This whole idea is reminiscent of the function of the Law for the Israelites. In the same way that Paul associates Jesus Christ with life, Moses associates Law with life:

> For I commanded you today to love the Lord your God, to walk in his ways, and to keep his commands, decrees and laws; then you will live and increase, and the Lord your God will bless you in the land you are entering to possess.[34]

---

[33] I Corinthians 12:12f (NIV).
[34] Deuteronomy 30:16 (NIV).

The Law represented a source of life for the Jews as Christ did for the Christians of the first century.

Besides Baptism, Paul uses the Lord's Supper as a source of identification with Jesus Christ. First of all, Paul describes the actual sayings of Jesus Christ. Paul recounts the Last Supper and Jesus' spoken words as a means to remind early Christians of the identification with Jesus Christ in a personal kinship, with the ritualistic partaking of "flesh and blood" of Jesus Christ as a symbolic establishment of that kinship. Paul writes:

> For I received from the Lord what I also passed on to you: The Lord Jesus, on the night he was betrayed, took bread, and when he had given thanks, he broke it and said, "This is my body, which is for you; do this in remembrance of me." In the same way, after supper he took the cup, saying, "This cup is the new covenant in my blood; do this, whenever you drink it, in remembrance of me." For whenever you eat this bread and drink this cup, you proclaim the Lord's death until he comes.[35]

In a society that valued kinship, a blood relationship, Paul shows Jesus Christ claiming social identification to himself of all believers using symbols of kinship -- blood and flesh.

---

[35] I Corinthians 11:23-26 (NIV).

For Paul, this identification with Jesus Christ is crucial; that is why Paul's account emphasizes remembering Jesus Christ more than the accounts given by the gospel writers. In I Corinthians 11, Paul attributes the statement, "Do this in remembrance of me," to Jesus of Nazareth in two points of the Last Supper. After breaking the bread, Jesus is recorded by Paul as saying: "This is my body, which is for you; do this in remembrance of me."[36] Also, taking the cup of wine, Jesus is claimed to have said: "This cup is the new covenant in my blood; do this, whenever you drink it, in remembrance of me."[37] This stands in contrast to the gospels. The gospels of Matthew and Mark do not mention Jesus as having said, "Do this in remembrance of me." The gospel of Luke does mention Jesus as having said, "Do this in remembrance of me." But it is only said in reference to breaking of bread. Jesus says: "This is my body given for you; do this in remembrance of me."[38] One can see that Paul was interested in emphasizing the remembrance of Jesus of Nazareth through the Lord's Supper, which functioned in the first century Mediterranean world in a very significant way to reorient the followers in a symbolic kinship with Jesus of Nazareth.

Paul feels that Lord's Supper, which brought symbolic identification of the believers in Jesus Christ, was so significant that he provides a warning in his directions for the participation in the Lord's Supper. Paul warns:

---

[36] I Corinthians 11:24b (NIV).
[37] I Corinthians 11:25b (NIV).
[38] Luke 22:19b (NIV).

> Therefore, whoever eats the bread or drinks the cup of the Lord in an unworthy manner will be guilty of sinning against the body and blood of the Lord. A man ought to examine himself before he eats of the bread and drinks of the cup. For anyone who eats and drinks without recognizing the body of the Lord eats and drinks judgment on himself.[39]

For Paul, the Lord's Supper provided a practical channel to emphasize identification with Jesus Christ.

In I Corinthians 10, Paul uses similar language of the body and blood to emphasize identification in Christ. But in contrast to I Corinthians 11, Paul uses the imagery of the body to expound on the significance of all believers' unity in Christ. Paul writes:

> Is not the cup of thanksgiving for which we give thanks a participation in the blood of Christ? And is not the bread that we break a participation in the body of Christ? Because there is one loaf, we, who are many, are one body, for we all partake of the one loaf.[40]

---

[39] I Corinthians 11:27-29 (NIV).
[40] I Corinthians 10:16f (NIV).

This participation in the body and blood of Christ has a redemptive value for Paul. He compares the table fellowship of the Christians with the sacrificial meal of the Israelites. Paul writes:

> Consider the people of Israel: Do not those who eat the sacrifices participate in the altar? Do I mean then that a sacrifice offered to an idol is anything, or that an idol is anything? No, but the sacrifices of pagans are offered to demons, not to God, and I do not want you to be participants with demons. You cannot drink the cup of the Lord and the cup of demons too; you cannot have a part in both the Lord's table and the table of demons.[41]

Paul is here equating the sacrificial meal of Israelites to Christian table fellowship. Sacrifice and sacrificial meal [42] was a central redemptive medium, which

---

[41] I Corinthians 10:18-21 (NIV). Much of the ancient world highly valued table fellowship. But it is interesting to compare Paul's emphasis of participating in the Lord's table and the Pharisaic concept that God was present at the table. Paul's emphasis on the Lord's table and his instructions on proper participation (I Corinthians 11:27-29) stands in contrast to Jesus' practice of Open Table Fellowship, in which he ate with "sinners and prostitutes." Jesus does not have requirements nor warning for his table fellowship.

[42] A. F. Rainey in his article "Sacrifice and Offerings," <u>Pictorial Encyclopedia of the Bible (Volume 5)</u>, ed. Merrill C. Tenney (Grand Rapids, Michigan: The Zondervan Corporation, 1976, pp. 194-211), writes that the central part of the peace offering was the communal meal. After giving the appropriate portion to

brought Israelites together as a covenant community. Paul attaches such redemptive value to Christian table fellowship, with the reason that it is participating in the body and blood of Christ, whom Paul describes as the "Passover lamb" in I Corinthians 5:7. One can see that Paul is symbolically depicting Jesus as a source of redemptive medium and identity for Christians.

Much of Paul's theology emphasizes redemptive identification with Jesus Christ. No passage is clearer in support of this than Galatians 3:26-29. Paul writes:

> You are all sons of God through faith in Christ Jesus, for all of you who were baptized into Christ have clothed yourselves with Christ. There is neither Jew nor Greek, slave nor free, male nor female, for you are all one in Christ Jesus. If you belong to Christ, then you are Abraham's seed, and heirs according to the promise.

---

the priest, the sacrificial animal was given to the offerer to be shared by him, his family, and the Levite in his community. Those participating in this meal had to observe strict ritual purity and eat in a designated sanctuary. Although rules were not as stringent for banquet meals, they in fact were sacrificial meals because the animals were ritually slaughtered at a local altar (208). For Israelites, these meals with food sacrificed to God identified the participants in the meal as members of the covenant community of God. Sacrificial meals were, therefore, a redemptive medium.

First of all, Paul starts out with the idea of being identified with Christ through baptism. He uses the prepositional "into" (εις) to describe the relationship of the person to Christ after baptism. The preposition denotes an intimate union with Christ. And these people, who have been baptized into Christ, are "clothed ... with Christ."

Non-Pauline passages do not use the imagery of clothing oneself with Christ. Both in the Old Testament and the non-Pauline New Testament, one can see that either the clothing is used in its usual sense with one's manner of dress or metaphorically with a concept, but never with a person. Old Testament passages employing the word "clothe" in all its permutations deal with either actual clothing/linen or concepts, such as splendor (Psalms 45:3; 104:1), strength (Isaiah 52:1; Proverbs 31:25), joy (Psalms 30:11), and righteousness (Job 29:14). Non-Pauline New Testament passages using the word "clothe" in all its permutations also deal with either actual clothing/linen or concepts, like humility (I Peter 5:5) and power (Luke 24:49). Paul shows his uniqueness in his use of the imagery of clothing to emphasize union with a person, Jesus Christ. Paul utilizes this imagery also in Romans: "Rather, clothe yourselves with the Lord Jesus Christ, and do not think about how to gratify the desires of the sinful nature."[43] Thus, one can see that Paul uses imagery of clothing normally associated with concepts to refer to Jesus Christ, a person, in order to provide a redemptive reference for believers.

---

[43]Romans 13:14 (NIV).

Furthermore, one can see from Galatians 3:28 that for Paul, identification with Christ and with other believers through the union in Jesus Christ was important and transcended cultural, ethnic, social, and gender boundaries. This was very much a part of Paul's thinking; for, he writes also in Colossians: "Here there is no Greek or Jew, circumcised or uncircumcised, barbarian, Scythian, slave or free, but Christ is all, and is in all."[44] One can see that it is important for Paul that there is unity among the believers with Jesus Christ as the reference point. For Paul, unity of the believers in Christ functioned as a redemptive medium. He uses redemptive language of Christians being "Abraham's seed" and "heirs according to the promise" to prove his point.

In conclusion, one can definitely trace in Paul's mind a stage on the road to hypostastic identification of Christ as the Law by the second century AD. Paul emphasizes unity with Christ and being in Christ. In doing so, Paul uses language and

---

[44]Colossians 3:11 (NIV). Although there is slight difference in language -- Galatians depicts believers as being in Christ but Colossians depict Christ as being in the believers -- in actuality, Paul is calling for unity in Christ in his letter "To the holy and faithful brothers in Christ as Colosse..." (Colossians 1:2a NIV). One can see this in Paul's exhortation to the Colossian believers, emphasizing their being in Christ. Paul writes: "So then, just as you received Christ Jesus as Lord, continue to live in him, rooted and built up in him, strengthened in the faith as you were taught, and overflowing with thankfulness" (Colossians 2:6f NIV). And Christian living is not merely in Christ, it is united in respect to other believers. Paul utilizes the imagery of the "one body": "Let the peace of Christ rule in your hearts, since as members of one body you were called to peace. And be thankful" (Colossians 3:15 NIV).

symbolism similar to those used in the Old Testament to describe the Law as redemptive medium, which provided the Jews with social and redemptive identity. For example, Paul uses Baptism to show that it is a source of life in the similar way the Law was. Also, the Lord's Supper functions in the redemptive way sacrificial meals did for Jews. Paul's theology concentrates on the redemptive identification of believers with Christ. This is nowhere more lucid than in Galatians 3:26-29. After examining Paul's thoughts in detail, one can be sure that, in a society where Paul's letters were constantly circulating, it was not difficult for the church fathers to hypostastically represent Jesus Christ as the Law. Paul had all but called Jesus the Law. He had provided redemptive significance of the Law in Jesus Christ.

Bibliography

Bailkey, Nels M. (ed.). 1992. *Readings in Ancient History: Thought and Experience from Gilgamesh to St. Augustine.* Lexington, Massachusetts: D. C. Health and Company.

Barrett, C. K. 1985. *Freedom and Obligation: A Study of the Epistle to the Galatians.* London: SPCK.

Bréhier, Émil. 1950. *Les idées philosophique et religieuse de Philon d"Alexandrie.* Paris: Librairie Philosophique J. Vrin.

Daniélou, Jean. 1964. *The Theology of Jewish Christianity.* Trans. John A. Baker. London: Darton, Longman & Todd.

Dunn, James D. G. 1990. *Jesus, Paul and the Law.* Louisville, Kentucky: Westminster/John Knox Press.

Mellor, Ronald (ed.). 1990. *From Augustus to Nero: The First Dynasty of Imperial Rome.* East Lansing, Michigan: Michigan State University Press.

Philo Judaeus. 1971. "On the Life of Moses." *The Essential Philo.* Ed. Nahum N. Glatzer. New York: Schocken Books, pp. 190-270.

Rainey, A. F. 1976. "Sacrifice and Offerings." *Pictorial Encyclopedia of the Bible (Volume 5)*. Ed. Merrill C. Tenney. Grand Rapids, Michigan: The Zondervan Corporation, pp. 194-211.

Sanders, E. P. 1983. *Paul, the Law, and the Jewish People*. Philadelphia: Fortress Press.

Tellenbach, Gerd. 1991. *Church, State and Christian Society at the time of the Investiture Contest*. Trans. R. F. Bennett. Toronto: University of Toronto Press.

Williamson, Ronald. 1989. *Jews in the Hellenistic World: Philo*. Cambridge, Great Britain: Cambridge University Press.

1984. *The Holy Bible: New International Version*. Colorado Springs, Colorado: International Bible Society.

"Investiture Contest as a Struggle for Right Order in the World: A Precis of Gerd Tellenbach's *Church, State and Christian Society at the Time of the Investiture Controversy*"[1]

The Investiture Controversy is one of the focal points of the Middle Ages. Scholars have given various interpretations concerning the cause, the nature, and the result of the Investiture Controversy from different angles. Gerd Tellenbach's *Church, State and Christian Society at the Time of the Investiture Contest* offers one explanation. Gerd Tellenbach sees the Investiture Controversy as "...a struggle for right order in the world" (Toronto: University of Toronto Press, 1991, p. 1). To explain what he means by this, Tellenbach sets the ideological, political, and religious scene around the time of the Investiture Contest, and then shows how some bright men in the Church succeeded in altering their present societal infrastructure through elaboration of the Church's ecclesiology.

What was the ideological scene like by the time of the Investiture Controversy? Gerd Tellenbach spends a lengthy section describing the different notions of freedom and hierarchy that came to shape the medieval understanding of these terms.

Tellenbach discusses the early Christian and the Roman concepts of freedom, which he believes,

---

[1] This paper was written in 1991. Professor Robert Benson, the medieval historian at UCLA, provided helpful comments.

provides the background for the medieval understanding of freedom and hierarchy. At first, early Christianity did not discuss freedom. This is evident in the Synoptic Gospels; they emphasized service, imitation, and surrender, rather than freedom. But after the Synoptic tradition, one finds Paul discussing the concept of liberty. Paul describes Christian liberty in terms of dependence -- away from lesser loyalty and toward God. Thus, a Christian, freed from sin, is no longer a slave to it, but rather a slave to righteousness and God. This is Christian freedom.

Augustine contributed to the shaping of the medieval understanding of freedom by elaborating on Paul's ideas. Augustine claimed that freedom can be increased or decreased depending on one's level of closeness in the relationship with God. In other words, there is a hierarchy of free beings. And those whose spiritual standing with God is hierarchically higher should be the ones who rule and guide those who are lower in their Christian freedom. This concept of hierarchy deriving from different levels of freedom had a great impact on the medieval understanding of the right order in the world.

The understanding of freedom under Roman Law, also, formed an important background for understanding the medieval concept of freedom. For the Romans, freedom referred to equal participation of all citizens in self-government and legislative action. Thus, the Romans dated freedom from the time of the absence of a monarch. Romans, however, had a *princeps*. But the Roman principate was no monarchy, at least in theory; the Roman people, corporately and in their freedom, entrusted power to the *princeps*.

This Roman understanding of freedom has some fundamental differences with the medieval understanding of it. Medieval thought did not conceive of transference of authority, as it was done in the Roman system to the *princeps*. Furthermore, the Roman concept of freedom is abstract in character. Roman Law is a boundary that encloses and protects an area which it does not occupy, which is, therefore, free. Thus, freedom imposes no limitations. In contrast to the negative limitation of the Roman concept of freedom, the medieval concept of freedom highlighted the positive elements of freedom. Therefore, *privilegium* and *libertas* are synonyms in the Middle Ages. Privilege does not refer to exemption from the law, but, like the medieval concept of freedom, it refers to complementary obligation of rights and duties. Because of this denotation, there are such things as privilege of land, of church, and of other inanimate objects. This kind of liberty, such as of a church, does not refer to its independence from lay authority or possession, but, rather, to its subjective right or the totality of subjective rights.

Furthermore, different understandings of law and of freedom provide for the fundamental difference in the status of a person in Roman times and in the Middle Ages. Despite the medieval emphasis on subjective rights, the free and the partly-free share in the same right, in that they both have concrete set of rights and corresponding duties, whereas in the Roman era a freeman is a person and a slave a thing. This is understandable in light of the medieval concept of natural law. God is the author of all law. Thus, there is no such thing as bad law; for, bad law is no law. Therefore, one discovers positive law, rather than making it. The positive law is sacred for everyone in the Middle Ages, but the law of the Romans provides freedom for those not under its dominion. In the Middle Ages, therefore, all are free; the only difference lies in the degree of freedom.

This leads into a discussion of hierarchy. In the Middle Ages, three different concepts of hierarchy were existent: ascetic, sacramental, and royal-theocratic views.

An ascetic, or monastic, conception of hierarchy emphasized withdrawal from the world and getting closer to God. Monks strove to win freedom by renouncing worldly ties and obligations. Their hope was in the life hereafter. Thus, they concentrated in storing up treasures in heaven by meritorious deeds on earth. Individual salvation was the aim of asceticism; there is little room for loving one's neighbor. What is really important is one's standing before God and that determines one's status in the heavenly hierarchy.

Unlike asceticism, a sacramental, or priestly, conception of hierarchy emphasized direct involvement in the world to bring people to salvation and participation in the sacraments. This view held that priests were representatives of Christ, who communicated to other humans the gift of Christ in which he is present; namely, the sacraments. As representatives of Christ on earth, priests held rank in the hierarchy of the Church according to the dignity of the task. But there was a distinction between the office and the person since priests were merely representatives of Christ; priests were not necessarily holy because they were consecrated.

The ascetic and sacramental views of hierarchy diverged at many points as shown above, but they both agreed that the laity were the lowest in the hierarchy. Those in the Middle Ages, however, did not hold in contempt the royal-theocratic view of hierarchy, which placed king at the top of the hierarchy. For, until the Investiture Controversy, the general consensus was that kings were different from other laymen. They had a special mission from God, and God manifests his will through them. Thus, at anointing, the king, or the emperor, is received into the ranks of the clergy as a symbol of the inner change. Furthermore, the king, as the ruler on earth, typified Christ, who ruled in Heaven. Therefore, many perceived the king as being on par with the bishop or even above him.

Among the three views, ascetic and royal-theocratic views were compatible because the ascetic life was not concerned with the world. But royal-theocratic and sacramental views were incompatible since both tried to exert their authority on earth. One could clearly see that the ideological stage was set for the struggle for the right order in the world.

How was the political and religious scene? Christianity transformed medieval society. Thus, three major elements were visible in the political and religious scene before the Investiture Contest; they are a royal theocracy, proprietary church system, and monastic piety.

Royal theocracy is the idea that the king is the servant of God, entrusted with the responsibility of protecting the Church and preserving its purity. Even before Christianity, ancients and Germanic people saw the king in a sacred way. Thus, it was not hard for those in the Middle Ages to swallow the concept of royal theocracy. In fact, they saw it as the norm. One can see that Visigothic, Anglo-Saxon, and Frankish kings perceived their position as an ecclesiastical one. Striking similarity between the consecration ceremonies and the ordination to episcopacy only reinforced their view. Also, the Church itself demanded from the state protection, provision for needs, and freedom from all burdens. Furthermore, because the consecration ceremony, as a sacrament dispensed by Christ alone, did not give superiority to the officiating bishop or pope, kings did not feel inferior to bishops or pope.

Because the German lords saw themselves as servants of God with the responsibility over religious matters, they set up proprietary churches in their estates and appointed priests of their own choice. Not all lords were moved by their religious conviction and obligation; some lords set up these proprietary churches only to collect tithes for personal gain. Whatever might have been the reason for building these *Eigenkirchen*, lords decentralized the Church through these proprietary churches and brought greater power to the lay lords, who became actively involved in religious matters through them. But on the other hand, these proprietary churches brought Christian religion, and along with that ecclesiastical organization, to the smallest strata of the society.

Besides royal theocracy and the proprietary church system, the Christian Church brought monastic piety to the medieval society. Monastic reformers avourab a strict rule for life after the Benedictine rule. Striving to be closer to God was of utmost importance to the monks. Monks concentrated on the life hereafter and ardently strove to store up treasures in heaven through good deeds. Monks also believed that one could acquire merit on behalf of others, including the dead. Gradually, those in the Middle Ages came to value monastic piety. Some lords expected only prayers from their *Eigenkloster*. Lords wanted their monks to pray and be close to God so that when they die, the monks could speak on their behalf. Through monks, people in the Middle Ages became more concerned with salvation and the afterlife.

Monastic piety went hand in hand with royal theocracy and a proprietary church system. Monasticism, which developed originally from the frustrated laity, differed from Sacramentalism in its view of the world. Therefore, it is not surprising to see conflicts arising when the bishops wanted to exert diocesan control over the monks, who wished exemption. The laity was on the side of the monks; therefore, until the third quarter of the eleventh century, monks could not and did not attack the secular power or the proprietary system.

In this atmosphere, Henry III stressed that government was a divine vocation. He strove to subjugate himself utterly before God, but also expected complete obedience from the populace on the basis that his will was divinely inspired. Then, Henry III called the synod of Sutri to elect a pope so that he would appear to fulfill his obligation as a theocratic king who watches over the affairs of the Church. But what this action ended up doing was to raise the awareness that there was something wrong about a layman possessing so much power over the Church. Thus, the political and religious stage was set for the struggle for the right order in the world.

The clergy realized that there was too much power in the laity. This sparked a struggle against the lay domination of the Church; namely, Investiture Contest. But efforts to alter the societal infrastructure did not see immediate success. This struggle was a gradual one, since royal theocracy was a concept that was widely accepted for a long time, even among the clergy. Furthermore, because popes themselves possessed large numbers of proprietary churches and monasteries, they did not make direct and explicit attacks on the proprietary system. But both lay and religious leaders tried to define and limit proprietary rights in the tenth and eleventh centuries.

After Bruno of Toul ascended as Pope Leo IX, he gathered around himself great personalities, like Hildebrand, Frederick of Lorraine, Humbert of Silva-Candida, Hugh the White and Boniface of Albano, who developed revolutionizing ideas. They became the pope's advisers as members in the curia. One of the greatly debated points in the curia was whether the orders of priests appointed by simoniacs were valid. But, as a matter of policy, the curia under

Pope Leo IX concerned itself with establishing the primacy of the bishop of Rome within the Church.

Wazo of Liège and the Auctor Gallicus took a step further. They had a clear perception of the dignity of the ecclesiastical hierarchy, especially that of papal dignity, and the fundamental difference between the spiritual and the temporal powers. Thus, Wazo criticized Henry III's calling the synod at Sutri to have a pope elected.

The death of Henry III and Pope Victor II within two years was what really accelerated the development of the Investiture Contest. The Churchmen disavowed promises they had made to Henry III and held papal elections themselves. After the election of Stephen IX as pope, they confirmed him with the approval of the German court. After Stephen IX's premature death, the Roman nobility held an election against the will of the cardinals. The Roman curia played the Romans against the German king by asking for approval of the choice of bishop Gerhard of Florence as pope.

The debates provoked by the political situation of 1057 and 1058 produced Humbert's *Libri adversus simoniacos*. Humbert attacked the position of the laymen in the church, especially the concept of royal theocracy. Humbert ignored the sacred nature of kingship; kings were simply laymen. The clergy should elect the bishops. Therefore, Humbert strongly objected to lay investitures.

But it was the sixth canon of the Easter synod of 1059 that outlined the program of the reformers. The emphasis was on keeping papal elections free from secular influences and on attaining free canonical elections everywhere. At first success was minimal, and it would take a hundred years before the new conception of canonical elections was understood and accepted everywhere. But one thing is certain; the Easter synod of 1059 opened the door for change – for the right order in the world.

But mere political action was not enough to alter the current societal infrastructure. There were beliefs that predominated the medieval society for hundreds of years. Total reorientation of thought was necessary to bring this about. This was done through the elaboration of the Church's ecclesiology.

The concept of the freedom of the Church was the matrix around which all arguments against the domination of the laity in the Church hung. For the Gregorians, a proper understanding of the freedom of the Church was crucial for gaining the right order in the world.

The Gregorians perceived the freedom of the Church in light of the freedom of God, which had no boundaries. They pointed to the close relationship between Christ and the Church to show that the Church shared in God's freedom. First, they pointed to the medieval idea that Christ is the head of the Church and the Church his body. Thus, when one restricts the freedom of the Church, one is affecting Christ, the head of the Church as well. Second, imagery of the relationship between Christ and the Church is that of bridegroom and bride, respectively. Medieval Christians, therefore, viewed the Church as the Mother Church. Christ and the Church are spiritual parents of every Christian. Therefore, it was important to protect the freedom of the Church on which salvation depended. This is why struggle against simony was a violent one. Simony made Church into a harlot. Anyone practicing it was the rapist of the bride of Christ. And simony in the time of the Investiture Controversy did not merely refer to exchange of offices for money, *simonia a manu*, but also to influencing the choice of the donor of offices by word, *simonia a lingua*, or by deed, *simonia ab obsequio*.

The bride and bridegroom imagery went further to include the clergy. The clergy as the representatives of Christ on earth and as the dispensers of the sacraments symbolized the bond between Christ and the Church; thus, they are also called head or husband of the Church in place of Christ. Simony was therefore a grave wrong. It hindered the freedom of the Holy Spirit. Also, lay rulers setting up clergy according to their will were acting as rapists of the Church. Because of the imagery of the clergy as the husband of the Church, the reformers attacked nicolaitism, neglect of celibacy by the clergy. Clergy who broke celibacy were not acting purely as the husband of the Church.

Besides the arguments against lay investiture, Gregory VII elaborated on the primacy of Rome and her pope as an important factor in ecclesiology that would provide the foundation for the establishment of the right order in the world. But Anonymous of York opposed the primacy of Rome by commenting that there was no such thing in the primitive Church. Although not everyone fully accepted the primacy of Rome, Gregory VII brought about papal monarchy and opened the door for papal domination.

The flip side of the emphasis on the primacy of Rome was the stripping of the supernatural, divine authority of kingship. Gregorians attempted to do this with propaganda: they made comparisons between spiritual and secular authority. They portrayed the spiritual authority in a more favorable light. For example, they compared spiritual authority with heaven and soul, whereas they portrayed secular authority as earth and body. Gregorians also made frontal attacks on the sacramental character of the Kingship. Gregory VII was, thereby, redefining ecclesiology without the supernatural characteristic of kingship. The royalists counterattacked with chapter thirteen of the Book of Romans, a chapter giving power to secular authority.

The Church may not have wiped out the concept of the supernatural character of kingship, but it did succeed in eliminating royal consecration from the sacraments of the church. Furthermore, when Henry IV condemned Pope Gregory VII, the pope retaliated by excommunicating him and deposing him, thereby symbolically separating the Church and state. Gregory VII put his newly defined ecclesiology in practice by his actions against Henry IV.

For Gerd Tellenbach, the Investiture Contest was a struggle for the right order in the world. By discussing at length the intellectual exercise, particularly on ecclesiology, and the background in which this exercise was done, Tellenbach shows that the Investiture Controversy was not merely a struggle over lay investitures, but an effort to develop a new mode of thought and to provide a new reference point for relating to the Church and the state. This is why

Tellenbach perceives Gregory VII as a great innovator in the history of Christianity.

About the Author

Heerak Christian Kim is Visiting Professor of Biblical Studies at Asia Evangelical College and Seminary in Bangalore, India. He has held many prestigious fellowships, including the Lady Davis Fellowship (1996-97), and has written many important academic books, including *Hebrew, Jewish, and Early Christian Studies: Academic Essays* and *Jewish Law and Identity: Academic Essays*.

www.ingramcontent.com/pod-product-compliance
Lightning Source LLC
Chambersburg PA
CBHW022059160426
43198CB00008B/289